D0893234

Dear reader:

The book of Nehemiah in the Old Testament is often used to illustrate principles of leadership, as the book's namesake demonstrated many such admirable qualities in spearheading the rebuilding of Jerusalem's walls. There are several very good books in print that expound upon this theme. When I first began reading the pages of this commentary on Nehemiah by my friend Stephen Davey, I inadvertently expected more of the same. I could not have been more pleasantly surprised at the depth and richness of what I found. Davey's insights leapt from the pages at me in sudden flashes of new understanding. In particular, I was convicted by the passages on prayer. I was also taken to new levels of understanding regarding Satan—what he can and can't do, and what we are to do accordingly. Immediately I knew this book was exactly right for subscribers to the All Grace Outreach series. It is with great pleasure that we present it to you now. May it be a rich blessing in your life and lead you ever more deeply into a faithful walk with Him!

Sincerely,

Chris Brady

Stephen Davey

WISDOM COMMENTARY SERIES

NEHEMIAH

CHARITY HOUSE
PUBLISHERS

Wisdom Commentary Series: Nehemiah

Author: Stephen Davey
Editor: Lalanne Barber
Cover Design and Body Layout: Grace Gourley
Photo of Stephen: Sam Gray Portraits, Raleigh, NC (samgrayportraits.com)
ISBN 978 0 9776641 7 7

Published by Charity House Publishers

Charity House Publishers, Inc.
2201 Candun Street
Suite 103
Apex, NC 27523-6412
USA

To my bride

~Marsha Anne ~

*without whom my life would have missed altogether
the companionship that creates so much love, music, and depth—
not to mention dreams that would never have seen the light of day.*

CONTENTS

The words of Nehemiah, the son of Hacaliah.
—Nehemiah 1:1

CHAPTER ONE

INTRODUCING AN ORDINARY MAN

Nehemiah 1:1

S ixteenth-century reformer Martin Luther once commented, "God created the world out of nothing. When I realize that I am nothing, perhaps God can create something out of me, too!"

Suppose you were to ask those who walk through the doors of a church on any given Sunday, "What kind of person does God use?" You would probably hear: "Somebody influential and talented" or "A uniquely gifted person with no obvious flaws" or "Extraordinary people, not regular folks like me."

Let me introduce you to a man who would *strongly disagree*. His name is Nehemiah, and by anyone's standards, he was a common, average, run-of-the-mill kind of guy. He maintained a good job and a steady income, but it would be completely accurate to describe him as an *ordinary* fellow. Yet the Old Testament book that bears his name will reveal how an *ordinary* man can be used in extraordinary ways when he is yielded to an eternal God.

VALUABLE JEWELS IN DARK COFFERS

One Christmas I gave my wife a beautiful bracelet. It came in an exquisite-looking black velvet box. The inside was lined in satin—the box alone was exciting. Why didn't I just wrap that bracelet in newspaper, twist the ends, and secure it with tape? Because somewhere in my life I had learned that the external packaging of a gift can enhance the beauty of what's inside.

It can highlight the luster and brilliance of the actual gift. When my wife opened that black velvet box, her heart was already prepared for something special.

Now, my wife never thanked me for the box, nor did she try to clasp it around her wrist. Without giving it a second thought, she set the box aside and fastened the bracelet on her wrist. The box had merely *prepared* her for the present inside.

Likewise, the beauty of Nehemiah's character and the luster of his testimony are all the more remarkable because of his *external* setting. Like the black velvet gift box, the scene in Nehemiah's day was a dark one. The Jewish people seemed to have adopted the motto, "National reformation will never happen again!" Humanly speaking, there was good reason for them to feel this way. They had been captives in a foreign land for many generations, and though Cyrus had declared them free to return to Jerusalem, two different attempts to leave (led by Zerubbabel and Ezra - *Ezra 2; 7*) had failed.

Consequently, the hearts and minds of the children of Israel reflected both grief and complacency during their days of captivity:

> *By the rivers of Babylon, there we sat down and wept, when we remembered Zion. Upon the willows in the midst of it we hung our harps. For there our captors demanded of us songs, and our tormentors mirth, saying, "Sing us one of the songs of Zion." How can we sing the LORD's song in a foreign land? If I forget you, O Jerusalem, may my right hand forget her skill. May my tongue cling to the roof of my mouth, if I do not remember you, if I do not exalt Jerusalem above my chief joy* (Psalm 137:1–6).

Talk about mournful lyrics! "In Babylon, we did not sing, but sobbed with grief. We had disobeyed our Lord, and we had ignored His Word, so we hung our harps on the willow trees. There is no singing, no music, no joy in Babylon. For how can we sing in a foreign land? How can we sing when the walls of Jerusalem are fallen? Even now that we are allowed to return and rebuild, our enemies are numerous. The task is impossible."

Against this despairing, overcast, solemn backdrop steps forth an ordinary man named Nehemiah. Empowered by God, he introduces the words to a new song: "It *can* be done!" But who is this man? His pedigree is brief:

The words of Nehemiah, the son of Hacaliah (Nehemiah 1:1).

Is that it? Surely there's more to be said about him, this man who's going to become the CEO of a huge—and I mean *huge*—project. But there were no other specifics, no qualifications, no interesting details to include. Nehemiah was not a member of Israel's priestly tribe; he didn't have royal blood in his veins; he was not a wealthy benefactor. In addition, Nehemiah lacked unusual physical strength and leadership experience. The phrase "Nehemiah, the son of Hacaliah" is another way of saying that Nehemiah is an ordinary, commonplace, everyday, average human being. There was nothing to be written about him signifying that he was outstanding or special. But

"God sees not as man sees, for man looks at the outward appearance, but the LORD looks at the heart" (1 Samuel 16:7).

THE VALUE OF THE BOOK OF NEHEMIAH

There are several benefits of studying this Old Testament book and the man for whom it is named:

- It gives us a timeless example of how God can make a *somebody* out of a *nobody*.

- It reveals what God can do with a person who yields his life to the will of His Father and doesn't have to receive the credit but gives any and all glory to Him.

- It removes any excuses that we may offer regarding our own inadequacies or inabilities.

The message comes in loud and clear: if God can use ordinary Nehemiah, He can also use you!

Frankly, the time is always ripe for a new reformer like Nehemiah. Burned gates are commonplace. There are demolished lives and wounded people everywhere. Values lie shattered, and morals are corroded. Every generation needs ordinary people who are willing to restore and rebuild broken and bruised people. Nehemiah is the kind of man whom God delights in using.

Today we have lost sight of what qualifies a man or woman for the role of restorer and rebuilder. Popularity, connections, personality, experience—these have all replaced the necessary characteristics that shine in the life of this ordinary man. The missing qualification that makes an ordinary person extraordinary is *character.*

> *"Roam to and fro through the streets of Jerusalem, and look now and take note. And seek in her open squares, if you can find a man, if there is one who does justice, who seeks truth"* (Jeremiah 5:1).

> *"I searched for a man among them who should build up the wall and stand in the gap before Me . . . but I found no one"* (Ezekiel 22:30).

God's qualifications for service are vastly different from ours. Consider the brilliant men who were living during the time of Nehemiah:

- Aristophanes was stirring people with his brilliant plays;
- Herodotus was captivating audiences with his best-selling history;
- Plato was influencing a generation of students;
- Socrates was brilliantly defining his philosophy.

Yet not one of *them* was selected by God to lead the Jewish people in the rebuilding of Jerusalem. The Apostle Paul gave insight into God's choice for reformers:

> *For consider your calling, brethren, that there were not many wise according to the flesh, not many mighty, not many noble; but God has chosen the foolish things of the world to shame the wise, and God has chosen the weak things of the world to shame the things which are strong, and the base things of the world and the despised, God has chosen, the things that are not, that He might nullify the things that are, that no man should boast before God* (1 Corinthians 1:26–29).

The Creator of all things chooses ordinary people who, like pliable clay, are molded in His hands to confound the wise and noble citizens of the world.

The memoirs of Nehemiah allow us to make a number of observations of the characteristics of the *ordinary* people God chooses and uses, which are reflected in his own life:

- He was compassionate.
- He prayed persistently—eleven prayers are recorded.
- He knew the Old Testament scriptures well.
- He had a definite goal for God's glory to be revealed.
- He went directly to the person when something had to be done.
- He depended on God to open doors of opportunity.
- He sized up the job before he started the work.
- He knew how to delegate work and responsibility.
- He refused to be stopped by external opposition.
- He knew how to settle differences between people.
- He was an example of his own message.
- He was a man of keen discernment.
- He did not let personal criticism slow him down.
- He did not excuse wrongdoing, regardless of who did it.
- He had respect for authority.
- He gave God the credit for accomplishments.
- He emphasized spiritual life.
- He required a higher standard for those in spiritual leadership.
- He refused to accommodate sin even when sinful behavior had become culturally acceptable.
- He took his personal distress and hurt to the Lord.
- He was willing to suffer injustice for the sake of God's work.
- He stayed focused on the goal and did not succumb to the dangers, the risks, the obstacles, or the hardships that stood in his way.
- He had moral strength and courage when everyone around him did not.
- He refused to give up, even when everyone else did.

How's that for a resumé that really matters?

Even a cursory reading of Nehemiah's memoirs reveals his integrity, his skillful use of the Word, and his consistency in reacting to the many injustices he received. The truth is we can read about these qualities and perhaps understand them, but *living* and *applying* them is not so easy. If we want to live like Nehemiah, we need to understand that this kind of life is only possible when we have a vital relationship with the one and only, true and living God. Perhaps this is why the memoirs of this man begin with him on his knees.

VALID QUESTIONS

Before we go too far into Nehemiah's journey, I urge you to ask yourself the following questions:

- Do you consider yourself ordinary?
- Do you consider yourself much more than ordinary?

Paul reminds us:

> *For through the grace given to me I say to everyone among you not to think more highly of himself than he ought to think; but to think so as to have sound judgment, as God has allotted to each a measure of faith* (Romans 12:3).

- Is there something in your life in need of repair?
- Is there something in your life in need of being rebuilt?

Before we begin this in-depth study of Nehemiah, make note of those broken things in your own life that God, the Master Rebuilder, needs to restore.

An elder in our church told me he never reads the Book of Nehemiah without asking what it is in his life that "lies in ruins." What a probing, life-changing question. Perhaps you identify more with Jerusalem's broken walls than with the man who will rebuild them. If that is the case, take comfort . . . God *can* and *does* restore the ruins of our lives. Nehemiah is a wonderful testimony to that fact.

And remember, if you think you have nothing special to offer God, take heart—Nehemiah is living proof that God delights in using *ordinary* people!

Hanani, one of my brothers, and some men from Judah came; and I asked them concerning the Jews who had escaped and had survived the captivity, and about Jerusalem. ³They said to me, "The remnant there in the province who survived the captivity are in great distress and reproach, and the wall of Jerusalem is broken down and its gates are burned with fire." ⁴Now it came about when I heard these words, I sat down and wept and mourned for days; and I was fasting and praying before the God of heaven.

—Nehemiah 1:2–4

CHAPTER TWO

WEEPING OVER HUMPTY DUMPTY

Nehemiah 1:2–4

There is a fascinating book in our public library titled *The Annotated Mother Goose*. It records the interesting history behind many popular children's rhymes. Although composed centuries ago, some of the rhymes and songs are still taught and memorized today. Take the story of Little Jack Horner, for instance.

Jack Horner was actually an employee of Richard Whiting, the last church leader or abbot of Glastonbury Cathedral in England. When King Henry VIII was taking over all the church property he could get his royal hands on, the abbot sent Jack Horner to London with a Christmas gift for the king. It was a delicious-looking pie. However, buried underneath the crust was anything but fruit: inside were hidden the deeds to twelve prestigious estates.

On the way to deliver the pie, knowing that the abbot was going to transfer these estates to the king, Jack Horner opened the pie and took out one of the deeds for himself. He chose the Manor of Mells, which was quite a "plum" piece of property. A number of years later, Jack Horner betrayed that same abbot by sitting on a jury which convicted him of embezzlement and then had him executed. That conveniently erased any possibility of the abbot telling the truth about King Henry VIII . . . and Jack Horner's family estate:

Little Jack Horner, sat in a corner,
Eating a Christmas pie.
He put in his thumb and pulled out a plum,
And said, "What a good boy am I."

Another chapter in this book unveiled the true meaning behind a children's game:

Ring around the rosies,
A pocket full of posies,
A-tishoo! A-tishoo!
We all fall down.

What is nothing more today than an innocent and fun little ditty was once a mournful death chant. It originated in seventeenth-century London during a plague of the Black Death. Each line of the rhyme was a reference to the plague:

- *Ring around the rosies* – the small, red, rash-like areas which appeared on the body of an infected person.
- *A pocket full of posies* – the superstitious belief that sweet-smelling flowers would drive off the demons who brought the disease. Therefore, they stuffed their pockets full of posies.
- *A-tishoo! A-tishoo!* – the constant sneezing which accompanied the plague.
- *We all fall down* – another way of saying we all die.

This nursery rhyme was actually a gloomy chant which expressed unbelievable sadness and fear.

Another interesting behind-the-scenes story was about an egg that fell and broke into so many pieces that it couldn't be reassembled:

Humpty Dumpty sat on a wall,
Humpty Dumpty had a great fall;
All the king's horses and all the king's men,
Couldn't put Humpty together again.

This was not a nursery rhyme about secret dealings with the king, the betrayal of friends, or the tragedy of a widespread disease. But it was, like the others, about human need and despair.

This rhyme first appeared in print in 1803. Humpty Dumpty was an egg, which explains why, having fallen off the wall and broken apart, he could not be put together again. However, eggs do not usually sit on walls. So what exactly did this wall-perched egg represent? For the original rhyme maker, Humpty Dumpty was intended to be a symbol of the origin of life and the world of humanity. It was designed to lament the fact that humanity had fallen and was broken, and not even the most powerful people on earth—the king himself, his army, nor his wise men—were able to put the broken pieces of life back together again.

One contemporary author wrote, "That's the world we live in . . . it specializes in producing broken people . . . and once broken, we discover that no power on earth can put us back together again."

The memoirs of Nehemiah happen to be a true story about broken things and broken people. They reveal deception and betrayal, as well as an epidemic of moral compromise and spiritual apathy. Much more than a bedtime story about a broken wall that gets fixed, it is the true life story of broken people who are restored by one ordinary man totally consumed with obeying God. A closer look will reveal a man whose ink well was often mixed with tears, and whose heart was broken over the condition of the city walls.

It is common when studying this book to race ahead to the prayer of Nehemiah in chapter one and skip past the fact that this kind of prayer emanated from the heart of a deeply burdened man. Certainly Nehemiah's prayer is a great model for the believer to follow. There are four steps on this wonderful path of prayer:

Adoration ➡ Confession ➡ Thanksgiving ➡ Supplication

Before you run off and practice these ACTS of prayer, you need to know one very important thing: they are only effective when they come from a heart that is first broken. The evidences of Nehemiah's broken heart are observed as he pleads:

> **"Let Your ear now be attentive and Your eyes open to hear the prayer of Your servant . . . O Lord, I beseech You, may Your ear be attentive to the prayer of Your servant"** (Nehemiah 1:6, 11).

Eleven times throughout his memoirs, Nehemiah pleads from a broken and passionate heart for the attention of God. Three times in the closing chapter, Nehemiah cries out, ***"Remember me, O my God."*** In fact, the very last phrase of his diary includes the words, "Remember me, O my God." This literally means, "Consider me; don't let my life ever leave Your gaze. O Lord, I want to be where You are; I want to go where You go; I want to walk where You walk; I surrender to think after and long after You; I beg of You to think after me."

This was the prayer of Nehemiah. He was a man who desperately wanted the maximum attention of God. Yes, he was an ordinary man, but he had an extraordinary desire for God. We get a glimpse into *who* Nehemiah was before seeing what he *did* through the power of God. He—and others like him—have discovered the truth of God's promise:

> *"And you will seek Me and find Me when you search for Me with all your heart"* (Jeremiah 29:13).

Since the entire earth is under the sovereign gaze of God, what does He mean when He implies that only those who "seek Him with all their heart" will receive His maximum attention? What did the writer of Hebrews mean when he said that God rewards those who diligently seek Him *(Hebrews 11:6)*?

It seems quite clear that although God sees everyone, He has a special communion reserved for those who want to see Him. While God already knows everything, He promises special blessing for those who really want to know Him! David wrote:

> *How blessed are those . . . who seek Him with all their heart* (Psalm 119:2).

The question remains: how, then, do we gain maximum fellowship *with* and maximum attention *from* God?

TAKING A CLOSER LOOK

The answer is in chapter one of the memoirs of a man who, though deeply troubled, stopped what he was doing and began weeping over the condition of Humpty Dumpty. Before Nehemiah ever began to rebuild, he first recognized the brokenness that no human power could remedy, and he then released his burden to the One whose power could resolve the problem.

Incidentally, the Hebrew name Nehemiah literally means *the consolation of God*. This average, yet consecrated, man will be used by God to live out the meaning of his name. Nehemiah will indeed bring the consolation of God, the relief of God, and the solace and encouragement of God.

What did he do in life? What was his occupation? The last part of **Nehemiah 1:11** tells us that he was a cupbearer. You could actually say that Nehemiah was the choice person in the entire kingdom to get close enough to the king to poison him if he so desired. The enemies of the king knew this fact and may have possibly offered Nehemiah wealth or greater position and power if he would join them in their attempt of a coup. Assassinations were a common occurrence, and at least two other biblical accounts shed light on the dangerous occupation of being a king:

- In the Book of Esther, Mordecai overheard the plans of an assassination attempt on the king's life and informed Esther *(Esther 2:22–23)*.

- *Genesis 40* records the time in Joseph's life when he was placed in a dungeon where he languished for years. Eventually, Pharaoh's baker and cupbearer were thrown into jail while an investigation took place to discover which of them was guilty of attempting to poison Pharaoh. You may recall that it was the baker who was found guilty and later executed, while the cupbearer was restored to his office.

So, the occupation of cupbearer was not only a common one to Old Testament kingdoms but also one sometimes enlisted to eliminate unwanted royalty. Zenophen, a student of Socrates, wrote, "Now it is a well-known fact that the cupbearer, when they offered the cup, would draw off some of it and swallow it down so that, if they should put poison in it, they may not profit by it."

Obviously, an Old Testament king trusted his cupbearer more than anyone else in his kingdom. This role involved more than handing the king his favorite drink. The Apocryphal book of *Tobit* recorded this of a man who was a cupbearer: "He was keeper of the signet ring and had charge of administration and of the accounts." Nehemiah, the cupbearer for Artaxerxes, was a trusted assistant to the most powerful man on earth. He was living in Persia with the king's cabinet in the palace of Susa—the winter resort of the kings. The palace and grounds covered five thousand acres, and precious gems and gold were part of the architecture. Murals of bulls with wings have been excavated and dated back to the times of Nehemiah. These murals were made with blue- and gold-painted bricks and must have been an incredible sight.

Being in the king's palace in Susa for the wintertime meant Nehemiah was in the middle of incredible affluence and power. He had worked hard to get this position. As a Jew in a foreign kingdom, he had achieved a trusted position in the realm. Even though he was of a different nationality, his occupation highly reflected his reputation for having godly character.

Remember that Nehemiah was worlds away from the broken-down city of Jerusalem. Indeed, the beloved city was four times smaller than this winter palace. Although Nehemiah himself was not rich, he was certainly in a place of comfort. Though an ordinary Jew, he had reached an unusual place of service before the Gentile emperor Artaxerxes.

TWO IMPORTANT QUESTIONS

Now it happened in the month Chislev, in the twentieth year, while I was in Susa the capitol, that Hanani, one of my brothers, and some men from Judah came; and I asked them concerning the Jews who had escaped and had survived the captivity, and about Jerusalem (Nehemiah 1:1–2).

Is this just polite conversation? No, he asked two specific questions and had a genuine concern to hear the answers:

1. What about the people?
2. What about the city?

His brother's answers would literally break the heart of Nehemiah:

And they said to me, "The remnant there in the province who survived the captivity are in great distress and reproach, and the wall of Jerusalem is broken down and its gates are burned with fire" (Nehemiah 1:3).

Why was this news so shocking to Nehemiah? After all, hadn't Babylon destroyed Jerusalem and left it in disarray many years ago? Yes, but he knew the walls were under construction during the return of exiles under the leadership of Zerubbabel and Ezra. However, what Nehemiah did *not* know was that the building project was forced to a halt by enemies of the Jews. Most scholars believe that enemies destroyed sections of the walls which had been partially reconstructed, according to *Ezra 4*. So, Nehemiah was asking, "Hey, how's it going under Ezra's leadership? How are the walls coming along?"

And the shocking reply: "Oh, Nehemiah, my brother, they've been torn down. The work has stopped, and the people have given up."

FIVE SYMPTOMS OF A BROKEN HEART

Now it came about when I heard these words, I sat down and wept and mourned for days; and I was fasting and praying before the God of heaven (Nehemiah 1:4).

Nehemiah privately recorded his response in his journal. This entry reveals to us five symptoms of a broken heart.

Contemplation

I sat down.

Evidently, Nehemiah took some time to think about and consider the report he had just heard. He did not merely hear the report with his ears . . . he heard it with his heart. He heard all that it implied, and he felt the anguish of those who were in distress. His normal, everyday, pleasant life became uncomfortable as he reflected on this disturbing news.

Compassion

I sat down *and wept*.

According to the April 1999 *World Monitor*, preschool teachers, administrators, and child development specialists said that the most important thing for a child to learn is self-reliance. They said that children should learn self-reliance seven times more than the educators who said children should learn sympathy and concern for others. The solution of educators would be to go out in the street and tell Humpty Dumpty, "Pull yourself together! We can't understand why you fell off that wall in the first place. Now, believe in yourself, stop sitting there, and get back on your feet!" Their version of the rhyme would go something like this:

Humpty Dumpty sat on a wall,
Humpty Dumpty had a great fall;
All of the scholars and their bright professors
Said, "Humpty, you've just got to get it together!"

This *self*-empowering philosophy says people are broken, and it is their responsibility to fix the broken pieces. They need to believe in themselves and have enough faith that they can do it. Any lack of self-confidence merely keeps them from "getting their act together." No wonder the last thing this popular philosophy would ever bother to teach children is the development of sympathy or empathy for someone else. However, that was not Nehemiah's philosophy. No, indeed! He sat down and wept for the broken people as well as the broken wall.

When was the last time you cried over your broken world? How long has it been since you wept over the crumbling circumstances someone else was facing?

Concern

I sat down and wept *and mourned for days.*

The word *mourned* is the Hebrew word *abal*. It literally means "to mourn for the dead." It is a deep, sorrowful mourning that does not soon pass away. It lingers on and on. We know from the text that Nehemiah will spend four months (from December [Chislev] until April [Nisan]) in this condition—four months lamenting the condition of the broken city and its brokenhearted inhabitants. E.M. Bounds, quoted in *A Passion for Faithfulness* by J.I. Packer, writes:

> How few the men in these days who can weep at the evils and abominations of the times! How rare are those who are sufficiently interested and concerned for the welfare of the church to mourn! Mourning and weeping over the decay of religion, the decline of revival power, and the fearful inroads of worldliness into the Church are almost an unknown quantity.

Concentration

I sat down and wept and mourned for days; *and I was fasting.*

This did not mean that Nehemiah took time off from work to go pray and maybe miss a few meals. Rather, this word *fasting* implies that he had completely lost his appetite. He was fasting simply because his burden was so consuming that it had taken away his desire to eat.

Communion

I sat down and wept and mourned for days; and I was fasting *and praying before the God of heaven.*

In the Scriptures, a number of different words are used for praying. Here, the Hebrew word involves pleading, deep emotion, and desperate lamenting before God. Nehemiah *must* hear from God . . . he *must* have God's maximum attention.

When we compare the date mentioned in chapter one to the date mentioned in chapter two, we learn that Nehemiah fasted, wept, mourned, and prayed for four months. Can you imagine weeping, mourning, fasting, and praying for *four hours*? What about *four days*? Can your mind conceive of fasting *four weeks*? Imagine: praying, weeping, mourning, and fasting for a period of *four months*. It is almost inconceivable, but his burden was just that heavy—his grief was that great.

John Knox, the Scottish Reformation preacher and leader, used to weep and pray in the royal gardens of Bloody Mary, the queen who hated the Protestant Reformation. Referring to John Knox, she said that she feared his prayers more than anything on earth. He would pray in her gardens loud enough for her to hear: "Oh God, give me Scotland, or I die."

Nehemiah had every reason not to be concerned with the condition of Jerusalem. Do not overlook the fact that he had been born in captivity and had never even been to Jerusalem, which means he had never worshipped in the temple. Frankly, he had a great career in Persia. He was at the king's right hand every day. Why would he ever pray, "Give me Jerusalem, or I die?" Why would he ever go to a broken-down city eight hundred miles away, to a people he did not know, and to a problem he did not create? Why? Because he was so burdened for the glory of God to shine from Jerusalem, for the people of God to be restored to honor, and for the inhabitants of that blessed land to worship the only true and living God! Serving the king his soup had suddenly lost its charm.

TOUCHING ON CRUCIAL LESSONS

There are two crucial lessons to apply from opening the pages of Nehemiah's memoirs:

1. If you want the maximum attention *of* God, you must first give your maximum attention *to* God. Do you want Him to be available to you? Are you available to Him? Do you want to move the heart of God? The question is can He move yours?

2. If you want the maximum blessing of God, you must be willing to receive the maximum burden from God.

So, just how stocked up are you on Kleenex . . . how willing are you to lose your appetite?

If you would like to volunteer to receive a burden for a broken-down world, here is what it looked like in ancient Babylon. The burden of Nehemiah had three distinct categories:

1. an *overwhelming concern* with an aspect of human distress or sin;

2. an *irresistible conviction* that God alone has the remedy;

3. an *unreserved compliance* in being willing for God to use him as part of the remedy.

In other words, if you are convinced there is a problem, you surrender to God to be a part of the solution. It is easier to pray, "Lord, do this . . . Lord, bless that . . . Lord, help him . . . Lord, move in this situation . . . Lord, deliver her." But what if we heard a voice from heaven saying that from the five requests we made, four of them were up to us? Are you willing to *be* the answer to the prayer? That is exactly the application of Paul's words to the Galatians when he commanded, *"Bear one another's burdens"* (Galatians 6:2). Nehemiah will bear the burden of a broken Jerusalem and a broken nation. Donald K. Campbell wrote in *Nehemiah: Man in Charge*, "A burdened God is at work in the world. He searches for burdened believers through whom He may work."

Is it shocking to you that the average Christian really does *not* want the maximum attention of God? What he really wants to do is get by with giving God *minimum* attention. He would rather someone else be part of the solution. After all, the problem is not really that bad.

Is it any wonder that we would rather play religious "games" for an hour or two on Sunday than set about to restore and rebuild broken lives? Acting concerned once a week does not require anguish over our own sin or the sins of others. Putting on our Sunday smile doesn't really mean we are available for God to hammer at our own hardened heart and then use us to build up some broken-down walls in someone else's world. The Sunday game rarely requires any commitment from us to set about repairing our broken world for Christ on Monday.

Let's rewrite this children's rhyme with a question for all of us:

> *Humpty Dumpty sat on a wall,*
> *Humpty Dumpty had a great fall.*
> *Do all the King's horses and all the Lord's men*
> *Care enough to put Humpty together again?*

Are you willing to have a broken heart over a broken world? If you are, you are now prepared to pray in the same way Nehemiah prayed.

You are prepared to gain the maximum attention of God.

I said, "I beseech You, O LORD God of heaven, the great and awesome God, who preserves the covenant and lovingkindness for those who love Him and keep His commandments, ⁶let Your ear now be attentive and Your eyes open to hear the prayer of Your servant which I am praying before You now, day and night, on behalf of the sons of Israel Your servants, confessing the sins of the sons of Israel which we have sinned against You; I and my father's house have sinned. ⁷We have acted very corruptly against You and have not kept the commandments, nor the statutes, nor the ordinances which You commanded Your servant Moses. ⁸Remember the word which You commanded Your servant Moses, saying, 'If you are unfaithful I will scatter you among the peoples; ⁹but if you return to Me and keep My commandments and do them, though those of you who have been scattered were in the most remote part of the heavens, I will gather them from there and will bring them to the place where I have chosen to cause My name to dwell.' ¹⁰They are Your servants and Your people whom You redeemed by Your great power and by Your strong hand. ¹¹O Lord, I beseech You, may Your ear be attentive to the prayer of Your servant and the prayer of Your servants who delight to revere Your name, and make Your servant successful today and grant him compassion before this man."

—Nehemiah 1:5–11

CHAPTER THREE

THE PRAYER PATH

Nehemiah 1:5–11

I am often asked the question, "How does prayer work?" My answer usually begins with the admission, "I don't know how prayer works; I just know that prayer *is* work! And those who work at prayer discover that prayer works."

If you were eavesdropping on Nehemiah while he prayed, you would get the strong impression that Nehemiah was certainly working at prayer. We have already discovered that Nehemiah understands the cost of a spiritual burden. He began his prayer by saying,

> *"[L]et Your ear now be attentive and Your eyes open to hear the prayer of Your servant"* (Nehemiah 1:6).

Does Nehemiah think that God is not listening? Does he think that God's eyes are not always open, that God is somewhat absent-minded about His universe? He continues his prayer,

> *"O Lord, I beseech You, may Your ear be attentive to the prayer of Your servant"* (Nehemiah 1:11).

Nehemiah's choice of words indicates that he does not want to take another step until he *knows* he has the intimacy, communion, and fellowship with God which is vital in rebuilding broken people. Before anyone can walk the path of restorer and rebuilder, they must first travel the path to God in prayer. The secret to Christian service is discovered in a private place—the intimate arena of prayer. What made Nehemiah successful in public before mankind was his successful private life before God.

FOUR STEPS IN THE PRAYER PATH

On November 19, 1863, Edward Everett, one of the most brilliant orators of his generation, stood to speak before a vast audience of American citizens. The press had come from around the nation to hear Everett and one other speaker dedicate a cemetery for Union soldiers killed in the Battle of Gettysburg. He spoke first, delivering an oration lasting one hour and fifty-seven minutes, interrupted periodically by cheering and thunderous applause from the mesmerized audience. A divided nation had come to this moment in history in desperate need of direction and healing following the bloodiest battle of the Civil War.

After Everett sat down, the second speaker stood, adjusted his wire-rimmed glasses, and proceeded to speak for two minutes, then sat down. A member of the Philadelphia press corps leaned over and whispered to him, "Is that all?"

He calmly replied, "That is all."

The next day, newspapers praised Edward Everett's speech and printed it on their front pages. Today, almost 150 years later, none of you knows one word of his two-hour speech, but most of you know some of that two-minute speech. It began with the words, "Fourscore and seven years ago, our fathers brought forth, upon this continent, a new nation, conceived in liberty, and dedicated to the proposition that 'all men are created equal . . .'"

The nation's newspapers gave the speech brief coverage. The socially elite found the remarks crude and insufficient. But over the course of time, Lincoln's Gettysburg Address became known for its depth and brilliance. Today it signifies a national desire for unity and freedom.

The following day, President Lincoln received a note from Edward Everett, thanking him for his kindness to him and his family at Gettysburg and commenting:

> I should be glad, if I could flatter myself that I came as near to the central idea of the occasion in two hours as you did in two minutes.

This story reminded me of another man who spoke on behalf of his divided, hurting nation. It is recorded for us in Nehemiah's personal diary. If you were to repeat his prayer from beginning to end, it would take less than two minutes. Yet, in those two minutes, Nehemiah delivered the central idea and gained the maximum attention of God. Have you ever wondered which prayer God listens to with great delight? How did Nehemiah—and how do we—invoke the attention of God? A close look at Nehemiah's prayer will reveal the essential PATH of prayer.

Priority of Sovereignty

"I beseech You, O LORD God of heaven, the great and awesome God" (Nehemiah 1:5*a*).

Prayer that gets past the living room ceiling is prayer that recognizes first and foremost that God is the Sovereign and man is the servant. Proper praying places God on His throne and mankind at His feet. Prayer is not our having our way with God—it is God having His way with us. Prayer is not our manipulating and controlling God but, rather God guiding and controlling us. Prayer is not an opportunity for us to pressure God but for God to pressure us.

Donald Grey Barnhouse once shocked his congregation by beginning a sermon on prayer with these words: "Prayer changes *nothing*." You could have heard a pin drop. His comment, of course, was designed to make Christians think about the sovereignty of God—that God is seated in the heavens and nothing ever surprises Him or falls outside His control. God cannot be bribed, cajoled, convinced, or impressed to change. Portions of recorded Scripture where God seemed to change His mind were actually part of His sovereign plan. He is unchangeable. To Barnhouse's statement, I would add that prayer changes nothing of God but *everything* of us. Therefore, if we do not want to be changed, we will not be praying effective prayers. Nehemiah began by praying, **"O LORD God of heaven"** (Nehemiah 1:5*a*).

The Lord Jesus taught His disciples to pray after the same model. The prayer in *Matthew 6:9* began with the words, *"Our Father who is in heaven."* Thus we observe this *same priority of sovereignty* introduced in the prayer of an Old Testament believer and taught as the prayer of New Testament believers.

The phrase "who is in heaven" or "O LORD God of heaven" is not so much a reference to God's address as it is to His attributes. "In the heavens" indicates His elevation above all creation. He is transcendent, majestic, and sovereign. Although we are allowed to come boldly to His throne of grace, we acknowledge His holiness and righteousness in all His ways.

That is what David understood when he wrote,

> *The LORD reigns, let the peoples tremble; He is enthroned above the cherubim, let the earth shake! Exalt the LORD our God and worship at His footstool; Holy is He* (Psalm 99:1, 5).

This has a way of reshaping your venture toward God because it reshapes your view of God.

This was the changing view of Job, who learned this about God:

- He thunders with His voice;
- He wears the clothing of dignity and eminence, honor and majesty;
- He commands the morning and makes the dawn to know its place;
- He laid the foundations of the earth and created its measurements;
- He enters the currents of the sea and walks the recesses of the deep ocean;
- He is the sovereign God who knows where the light lives and the way of the east wind;
- He is the One who has created the purposes of floods and thunderbolts, ice and hail;
- He leads forth the constellations; He determines the orbits of planets;
- He counts the clouds and tips the water jars of heaven;
- He has created the animals with their instincts;
- He is the One who has spread the heavens like a mirror;
- He is the One exalted in power and surrounded by majesty.

Is this the kind of God whom you approach?

This God is not a genie who will give you three wishes if you rub hard enough on the prayer lamp. He is not a doting grandfather with lollipops in his pockets. He is not, as one man called Him, "a gumball machine" into which you insert your prayer quarter and get a bubble gum ball. This One is seated in the heavens. This One is both loving and terrifying. He is both gracious and holy. He is merciful and, at the same time, just.

As you pray, picture Him high and lifted up on His great majestic throne with angels hovering about Him chanting continuously, "Holy, holy, holy . . ." Then you will be seeing Him as Nehemiah saw Him—***the great and awesome God***. J.I. Packer wrote in *A Passion for Faithfulness* that Nehemiah "had grasped the greatness of God."

The **proper perspective** leads to a **proper priority** of God's sovereign ownership and control. Therefore, you can say to God: "You reign over all creation; You rule over all that is. Indeed, You order every detail of my life. You are completely capable, totally trustworthy, and full of wisdom. In awe, I enter Your marvelous presence and bow before Your majestic throne."

I can still remember my fifth grade teacher asking me to stay after class and come to his office for an appointment. Realizing that my previous after-school meetings had not been pleasant occasions made a wave of fear sweep over my body. Fortunately, this time the teacher said he wanted to sit down and discuss something of importance to the fifth grade class and, specifically, wanted to talk over the matter *with me*. This was truly meaningful because most of the fifth grade boys admired this tall, strong, deep-voiced, gracious man who, incidentally, always smelled like coffee. I remember how important I felt going into his little office, sitting in the chair, and having that appointment with him. I went there with confidence because he had invited me, but there was also trembling because of who he was. And I remember saying, "Yes, sir," a lot!

Proper praying balances boldness with reverence. We have been invited into God's presence and we approach with confidence because we were invited, yet, with trembling because we are aware of Who has invited us. We tend to say, "Yes, Father," a lot.

We would never say, "Now listen here, let me tell You my view on the matter," or "I think You're going about this all wrong." Proper praying places God on His throne and mankind at His feet.

David wrote in Psalm 145, *I will extol You, my God, O King.* The word *extol* comes from a Hebrew word which means "to lift high, to raise up." David continues singing:

> *And I will bless Your name forever and ever. Every day I will bless You, and I will praise Your name forever and ever. Great is the LORD, and highly to be praised, and His great-*

ness is unsearchable. One generation shall praise Your works to another, and shall declare Your mighty acts (Psalm 145:1*b*–4).

On the glorious splendor of Your majesty and on Your wonderful works, I will meditate. Men shall speak of the power of Your awesome acts, and I will tell of Your greatness. They shall eagerly utter the memory of Your abundant goodness and will shout joyfully of Your righteousness. The LORD is gracious and merciful; slow to anger and great in lovingkindness. The LORD is good to all, and His mercies are over all His works. All Your works shall give thanks to You, O LORD, and Your godly ones shall bless You. They shall speak of the glory of Your kingdom and talk of Your power; to make known to the sons of men Your mighty acts and the glory of the majesty of Your kingdom (Psalm 145:5–12).

Prayer does not begin with the believer going into the presence of God and saying, "Lord, here I am," but instead, saying, "O sovereign Lord, there *You* are." Prayer is not the *communication* of our will but the *surrender* of our will to God. And as we will see in the life of Nehemiah, good praying does not result in our having our way with God but in God having His way with us.

When our Lord Jesus taught His disciples to pray, He said, *"Whatever you ask in My name, that will I do"* (John 14:13*a*). Many people like to claim and quote this verse, but not too many keep reading the rest of the verse: *"that the Father may be glorified in the Son."* Most of us end our prayers by saying, "In Jesus' name, amen." This *is* a biblical thing to say. After all, we are going to God by the authority of our great High Priest Jesus Christ. However, we must remember that to pray in Jesus' name means that our prayer should be one to which the Lord Jesus would not hesitate to sign His name. Prayer that receives Christ's signature is prayer that recognizes the glory, majesty, will, and design of the Father. Nehemiah wholeheartedly recognized the priority of God's sovereignty, and it became the first stepping stone on his path of prayer.

Acknowledgement of Sin

The prayer PATH not only requires the priority of sovereignty, but it also includes a second step: a contrite acknowledgement of sin.

The reason we take this second step is because we have already taken the first step. Therefore, we cannot tolerate sin in our lives because we understand God's sovereignty over our lives. Isaiah saw a vision of God's glory and immediately confessed:

> *"I am a man of unclean lips, and I live among a people of unclean lips"* (Isaiah 6:5).

Paul progressed in his own spiritual walk with Christ and, near the end of his life, he remarked in a letter to Timothy concerning *sinners, among whom I am foremost of all* (1 Timothy 1:15).

A person who does not embrace God's sovereignty will never acknowledge personal sin, and the path of prayer is cut short of all its rich benefits:

> *"[L]et Your ear now be attentive and Your eyes open to hear the prayer of Your servant which I am praying before You now, day and night, on behalf of the sons of Israel Your servants, confessing the sins of the sons of Israel which we have sinned against You; I and my father's house have sinned"* (Nehemiah 1:6).

Notice the pronouns *I* and *we*. He does not say, "Oh, Lord, let me tell you what *they've* done. Man, did my forefathers mess up everything." No, Nehemiah admitted, *I and my father's house have sinned.* Perhaps for the first time, Nehemiah was struck by the fact that he was not supposed to be in Susa—he was supposed to be in Jerusalem. He refers to the covenant in verse five and then elaborates on it in verses eight and nine. He calls God by His covenant-keeping name Yahweh. The covenant with Yahweh that he refers to is the Palestinian Covenant, which we will examine later. But for now, he begins to confess with a full understanding that he was not where he was supposed to be. He did not belong in the palace; he belonged in Palestine.

Do you want the maximum attention of God? Then, can you acknowledge your sin to God? Notice he did not say, "Lord, I've made a few mistakes recently; I really messed up today . . . You know me and my indiscretion. You probably heard me tell that little white lie; You know how flexible my expense accounts are, and I suppose you saw my little episode of righteous indignation. Lord, you know how I am . . ."

God does not forgive *excuses*—He forgives *sin*. But I challenge you not to stop with the word *sin*. If you have trouble just saying that little word, you will probably not be able to confess the actual thought, word, or deed. Nehemiah didn't simply make a blanket confession of sin, he *named* each offense:

> **"We have acted very corruptly against You and have not kept the commandments, nor the statutes, nor the ordinances which You commanded Your servant Moses"** (Nehemiah 1:7).

"We are guilty of sin—specifically: corruption, disobedience, and breaking God's law." Did he leave anything out?

The people who know how to gain the maximum attention of God are people who know they are sinners and utter no escape clauses in their prayers. David wrote in his prayer of confession:

> *The sacrifices of God* [the sacrifices that really get God's attention] *are a broken and a contrite heart* (Psalm 51:17).

Brokenhearted people are used by God to restore a broken world. Why? Because they have come to see His greatness and have come to admit their own guilt. They have caught a fresh glimpse of His sovereignty and their own sin and have admitted to both. Do you admit His sovereignty and your sin? Do you then confess your sin and submit to His sovereignty? To those who do, the Bible promises:

> *If we confess our sins, He is faithful and righteous to forgive us our sins and to cleanse us from all unrighteousness* (1 John 1:9).

Recently, my wife came home from the grocery store with the kind of beef hot dogs that we like. They have no fillers, no by-products, no artificial coloring, and no added flavors. This way we know that we aren't eating something collected off of the nearby highway. The brand that Marsha brought home was Hebrew National Kosher Beef Franks. As we were eating those

Kosher dogs, she read aloud this quote from the front of the package: "We answer to a higher authority." Then, on the back, another paragraph read,

> You've heard the word *kosher*, but did you know that it literally means "fit to eat"? Hebrew National must follow strict biblical dietary laws, use only certain cuts of kosher beef, and meet the highest standards for quality. For over 95 years, our commitment to manufacturing products of only the highest quality means that artificial by-products are simply not allowed. Kosher also stands for quality and goodness, and that's why we believe our franks taste so superior. Hebrew National answers to a higher authority—so that you can enjoy the best.

Isn't that great! Imagine a company so convinced they answer to a higher authority that this belief completely governs the way they make hot dogs. Oh, if only every Christian lived as if stamped upon his hands, feet, and heart were the words, "I answer to a higher authority; I am accountable to a higher Holy Being; when I go to Him in prayer, I do not tell Him anything; I answer to Him for everything." We truly *do* answer to a higher authority. Even those who refuse to answer to Him now will ultimately have to at the Great White Throne or at the Judgment Seat of Christ.

Unfortunately, there are those who do not acknowledge their sin before God. In fact, two categories of people are listed in Scripture as ones to whom the Great Sovereign turns a deaf ear.

1. Unbelievers

Part of the strategy of Satan, as well as the deception of the human heart, is to make people believe that they can refuse the truth of the Gospel of Christ and yet still have access to God. Polls reveal that twice as many people pray to God than believe in the Gospel of Jesus Christ.

Just ask them for yourself: "Do you pray to God?"

"Sure, I pray to God! He even answers some of my prayers."

"But do you believe in Jesus Christ?"

"Well, now you're getting too fanatical!"

The Bible clearly and emphatically states:

"We know that God does not hear sinners; but if anyone is God-fearing, and does His will, He hears him" (John 9:31).

In the Old Testament, the same thought is given when David writes:

The eyes of the LORD are toward the righteous, and His ears are open to their cry . . . The righteous cry, and the LORD hears" (Psalm 34:15, 17*a*).

The word translated *righteous* has to do with one's standing before God, not one's perfection before men. Paul tells us that we have the righteousness of Christ, having placed our faith in *Him alone (1 Corinthians 1:30)*. The first prayer an unbeliever speaks that God listens to is the prayer of repentance and the request for personal salvation through Jesus Christ *alone*.

2. Disobedient Believers

If I regard wickedness in my heart, the LORD will not hear . . . my prayer (Psalm 66:18, 19*b*).

Does that mean that you cannot pray unless your heart is sinless? No—if that were the case, none of us could ever pray. The word *regard* means *to cherish and defend*. In other words, "If I cherish and defend sin in my heart, God will not hear me." You can go ahead and pray, but God will not be acknowledging your prayer.

Peter became even more specific for the New Testament believer when he wrote these startling words:

You husbands . . . live with your wives in an understanding way . . . so that your prayers may not be hindered (1 Peter 3:7).

For married men, your relationship with your wife is either an obstacle or an aid to your prayer life. In other words, if you are a married man, one of the best ways to get God's attention is to give your wife your attention. Isn't it fascinating to think that your fellowship with others on earth affects your fellowship with God in heaven?

David said:

I acknowledged my sin to You, and my iniquity I did not hide . . . and You forgave . . . my sin (Psalm 32:5).

In his prayer that gained God's maximum attention, Nehemiah admitted:

> *"I and my father's house have sinned. We have acted very corruptly against You . . ."* (Nehemiah 1:6b–7).

Prayer that gains the maximum attention of God is prayer that places a priority on God's sovereignty and also acknowledges personal sin and guilt.

Trust in the Scriptures

Did you know that the Bible is not so much a book of answers as it is a book of promises? In chapter one, Nehemiah repeats from memory at least ten different passages from the Law of Moses, which records the promises of God to His people Israel. In **Nehemiah 1:5**, he offers his prayer to Yahweh, which is His covenant-keeping name. This name refers to the burning bush encounter when God told Moses that he was going to lead the children of Israel out of Egypt into a land flowing with milk and honey *(Exodus 3)*. Moses' response, in effect, was "I don't think they're going to believe that; they will probably ask me *what* god gave such an unbelievable claim." In answer to Moses' disbelief, God told him the name of the God issuing such an astounding promise: *"I AM WHO I AM"* (Exodus 3:14). I AM is the Hebrew verb *hayah*, and Yahweh is the name derived from that verb. Yahweh is the name Nehemiah refers to because that name represented the promise of God and the promise-keeping nature of God. So, from the beginning of Nehemiah's prayer, he is subtly saying, "You are the God who keeps Your covenant promise."

However, the next promise Nehemiah claims will eliminate subtlety altogether!

> *"[W]ho preserves the covenant and lovingkindness for those who love Him and keep His commandments"* (Nehemiah 1:5).

This is a paraphrased quotation from *Exodus 20:6*, where God promised Moses that He would show *lovingkindness to thousands, to those who love Me and keep My commandments*. Nehemiah is literally claiming the promise of God made centuries earlier from Mount Sinai when he prays,

> *"Remember the word which You commanded Your servant Moses"* (Nehemiah 1:8a).

Then, he claims another promise recorded in *Leviticus 26:33* by directly quoting the words of God to Moses:

"'If you are unfaithful I will scatter you among the peoples'" (Nehemiah 1:8*b*).

Still quoting from memory, this time from *Deuteronomy 30:2, 4,* Nehemiah prays:

"'[B]ut if you return to Me and keep My commandments and do them, though those of you who have been scattered were in the most remote part of the heavens, I will gather them from there and will bring them to the place where I have chosen to cause My name to dwell'" (Nehemiah 1:9).

Nehemiah is effectively pleading, "Listen, O covenant-keeping God! You promised that if we were unfaithful, we would be scattered—and You kept that promise. Now, would You please keep Your promise that if we return to You, then You will restore us to the place where Your name dwells?" In the very next verse, Nehemiah simply repeats to God a paraphrase of *Exodus 32:11,* where Moses also interceded for the rebellious people of Israel. So, like Moses of old, Nehemiah now prays:

"They are Your servants and Your people whom You redeemed by Your great power and by Your strong hand" (Nehemiah 1:10).

Here's the point: the majority of Nehemiah's prayer was the reciting and paraphrasing of Scripture. His prayer was filled with the promises of God in His Word. **Nehemiah had grasped the Word of God, and now the Word had a grip on him.** He had evidently been through the Old Testament many times, and now the Old Testament was coming out through him.

How important are God's promises to you? The reason we believe in heaven is because we are promised that we have *eternal life, which God, who cannot lie, promised long ages ago* (Titus 1:2*b*). The reason we believe that godly living is possible is that God promised that we have *everything pertaining to life and godliness, through the true knowledge of Him who called us by His own glory and excellence* (2 Peter 1:3*b*). We can approach God in prayer because the Bible has assured us that we can confidently *enter the holy place by the blood of Jesus* (Hebrews 10:19). Could it be that we do not know what to say to God in prayer because we do not know what He has already said to us in His Word? Could it be that we live fearful, anxious lives because we have forgotten the promise that Christ intercedes on our behalf?

Charles Swindoll, in his book *Tale of the Tardy Oxcart*, quoted Robert Murray McCheyne as saying more than one hundred years ago: "If I could hear Christ praying for me in the next room, I would not fear a million enemies. Yet distance makes no difference, He is praying for me even now." Would *you* like that confidence? Nehemiah had it! He knew what to say because he knew what the Word had already said.

Humility in Supplication

This is the final, foundational stone necessary to lay a clear PATH to God. The prayer that gains the maximum attention of God is the prayer that has all four stones in place: the **P**riority of Sovereignty, an **A**cknowledgment of Sin, a **T**rust in the Scriptures, and **H**umility in Supplication.

> *"O LORD, I beseech You, may Your ear be attentive to the prayer of Your servant and the prayer of Your servants who delight to revere Your name* [Nehemiah's humility is expressed here] *and make Your servant successful today and grant him compassion before this man* (Nehemiah 1:11).

It is insightful that the *last* thing Nehemiah prayed was a request. Chapter two will give us the details of what Nehemiah had in mind. But did you notice in this verse that Nehemiah is personally volunteering to become a part of God's solution to the problem in Jerusalem? Have you discovered yet that the greatest thrill in praying is not necessarily in receiving an answer but in *becoming* the answer?

One author retold a news story that occurred several years ago.

> A young man had come from Korea to Philadelphia to attend a Christian college in the United States. He graduated and continued to earn a master's degree from the University of Pennsylvania. One night as he went to mail a letter, he was held up by some teenage boys who demanded his money. The young thugs became angry because he didn't have a lot of money, and they proceeded to actually beat him to death. Later, the Philadelphia police caught and arrested them. Their

trial received international attention; the victim's family flew to the States to attend. At the conclusion of the trial, the boys were found guilty of murder.

Prior to the passing of the sentence, the parents asked if they could say a word. Then, before a packed courtroom, this Korean mom and dad got down on their knees in front of the judge and asked him to allow them to take these boys who killed their son back to Korea. They explained that these young men needed the love of parents and the love of Christ. The judge didn't have that kind of authority—he explained to them that American jurisprudence would not allow this. While they were denied their request, their testimony shone brilliantly in a dark, broken-down world.

How many of you have gone to your knees before your great and holy Judge—the God of heaven and earth, the God of mercy, the God of justice—and pled for a broken world . . . prayers that focused on something besides yourself, your life, your problems, your aches and pains, your needs—and volunteered *your very own life* as a solution? Do you want to make a difference? Do you want to become part of the solution in rebuilding a broken world? If so, you will need the maximum attention of God which comes from praying along the prayer PATH.

You begin with the priority of the sovereign majesty of God; then ask Him to break your own heart and to acknowledge your own sin; lean heavily and entirely in your trust upon the promises of His Word. And end in humility, with the submission of your own available life.

Prayers like these don't have to last for two hours; they can be two minutes or less.

When you pray like Nehemiah prayed, you can, with confidence, end your prayer by saying those wonderful words, "In Jesus' name, amen."

And it came about in the month of Nisan, in the twentieth year of King Artaxerxes, that wine was before him, and I took up the wine and gave it to the king. Now I had not been sad in his presence. ²So the king said to me, "Why is your face sad though you are not sick? This is nothing but sadness of heart." Then I was very much afraid. ³I said to the king, "Let the king live forever. Why should my face not be sad when the city, the place of my fathers' tombs, lies desolate and its gates have been consumed by fire?" ⁴Then the king said to me, "What would you request?" So I prayed to the God of heaven. ⁵I said to the king, "If it please the king, and if your servant has found favor before you, send me to Judah, to the city of my fathers' tombs, that I may rebuild it." ⁶Then the king said to me, the queen sitting beside him, "How long will your journey be, and when will you return?" So it pleased the king to send me, and I gave him a definite time. ⁷And I said to the king, "If it please the king, let letters be given me for the governors of the provinces beyond the River, that they may allow me to pass through until I come to Judah, ⁸and a letter to Asaph the keeper of the king's forest, that he may give me timber to make beams for the gates of the fortress which is by the temple, for the wall of the city and for the house to which I will go." And the king granted them to me because the good hand of God was on me. ⁹Then I came to the governors of the provinces beyond the River and gave them the king's letters. Now the king had sent with me officers of the army and horsemen. ¹⁰When Sanballat the Horonite and Tobiah the Ammonite official heard about it, it was very displeasing to them that someone had come to seek the welfare of the sons of Israel.

—Nehemiah 2:1–10

CHAPTER FOUR

THE REAL McCOY

Nehemiah 2:1–10

Late one night around 1840, two slaves from Kentucky slipped out of their shack and into the darkness. This husband and wife left the plantation and were soon on their way to freedom as the newest passengers on the Underground Railroad. Moving from safe house to safe house, they made their journey to the "promised land" of freedom. They did not stop until they reached Canada.

They had a son in 1843 and named him Elijah. When he was three years old, the family moved back to the US, settling in Detroit. He was able to attend school near his home, while his father prospered in business ventures. Because of his father's success, he sent Elijah to Edinburgh, Scotland, where he served a mechanical engineering apprenticeship. Returning to Detroit, he was unable to find work in his field but landed a job as a fireman and oiler on the Michigan Central Railroad. At that time, trains needed to stop periodically and be lubricated. Recognizing the need for a better system, Elijah designed a lubricator for steam engines that didn't require them to stop. He secured a US patent for his lubricator cup.

Elijah didn't stop with that, though. He kept improving his device and developed variations of it. He adapted it to other machinery and, in time, received forty-two patents for inventions in lubrication systems, as well as other patents for need-based tasks, such as a portable ironing board and a lawn sprinkler.

There were others who tried to copy his work, but his inventions were so superior that people would settle for nothing less than the original by Elijah

McCoy. Today, people who will not be satisfied with a substitute, a knockoff, or an imitation want "the real McCoy."

Having studied the life of Nehemiah, I have come to the conclusion that he was the real McCoy: a genuine, authentic follower of God. The biblical book that bears his name is as real as he was. Through his memoirs, we are allowed to observe not only the strengths of Nehemiah but his weaknesses. We are able to watch him when he is fearless and courageous—and when he is weak and afraid. We will discover both sides of this great man as we study chapter two. In the verses ahead, we see no façade, no pseudo-spiritual language, no false piety but, rather, the real McCoy of faith.

A SUDDEN OPPORTUNITY

And it came about in the month Nisan, in the twentieth year of King Artaxerxes, that wine was before him, and I took up the wine and gave it to the king. Now I had not been sad in his presence. So the king said to me, "Why is your face sad though you are not sick? This is nothing but sadness of heart." Then I was very much afraid (Nehemiah 2:1–2).

Remember that Nehemiah has been pouring out his heart to God for four months. He has been fasting, weeping, and praying about the condition of Jerusalem and has been asking God to use him to rebuild the city. Yet up to this point, he has been able to keep his burden a private matter while he waited for an answer from God. No one, including the king, has been able to observe the agony Nehemiah has been feeling. But all of that changes when Nehemiah inadvertently lets his feelings show. He is surprised to hear the king ask, "Why this sadness of heart?"

You would think that this would be an invitation from Artaxerxes for Nehemiah to sit down on the couch and say, "Well, Art, old buddy, nice of you to ask." Why would Nehemiah write, *"I was very much afraid"*?

Remember, Nehemiah's job was to protect the king from any assassination attempts through poisoning: wine in his goblet or the addition of something deadly to his casserole. Any change in Nehemiah's behavior or countenance would arouse suspicion from an already paranoid king whose own father had been assassinated. Furthermore, you can actually translate the word *sadness* a different way: "Why is your face troubled with evil?" In essence, the king says, "Nehemiah, something is wrong. What's going on here?"

> *Then I was very much afraid. I said to the king, "Let the king live forever.* [That's another way of saying, "There's nothing in your drink, O King—I promise!"] *Why should my face not be sad when the city, the place of my fathers' tombs, lies desolate and its gates have been consumed by fire?"* (Nehemiah 2:2*b*–3).

For four months Nehemiah has been asking God to grant him favor in the eyes of the king so he might return to Jerusalem. This is the same king who, in *Ezra 4*, ordered the work stopped. God would have to do something really unusual to change his heart. So Nehemiah has been fasting and praying, "O God, grant me a favorable audience with the king." Then suddenly—unexpectedly—Nehemiah let the anguish of his heart show on his face for just a moment. The king immediately noticed and demanded an explanation. Nehemiah somewhat hesitantly replies, "I'm sad because my father's city lies desolate, and its gates are burned with fire." I wonder if Nehemiah thought to himself, *That's not the way I wanted to say it. No, that did not come out right at all!*

Have you personally found that no matter how long you plan, you can never plan enough for the unexpected? I doubt Nehemiah would have picked this day or this way to bring up the subject. He is now on the defensive, and the king is suspicious. This is not the way he planned it to happen. Now he is afraid.

The real McCoy of authentic Christianity is not the person who is self-assured, always together, never afraid. Rather, it is the person who is caught off guard, filled with fear and trembling, unsure of himself and, as we will see in a moment, totally dependent upon the strength of God.

A SURPRISING REQUEST

> *Then the king said to me, "What would you request?"* (Nehemiah 2:4*a*).

Nehemiah's head had to be spinning! Notice he has not asked the king for anything; he simply told the king why he is troubled. But something is moving the heart of the king to discern what he has not heard: Nehemiah wants to ask him for a favor. Who do you think was moving the heart of the king? Another king named Solomon answers:

> *The king's heart is like channels of water in the hand of the LORD; He turns it wherever He wishes* (Proverbs 21:1).

A SHORT PRAYER

So I prayed to the God of heaven (Nehemiah 2:4*b*).

This is one of those silent, quick, SOS prayers! But remember, it is not the length of the prayer that is important—it is the Person to whom Nehemiah is praying: the God of heaven. We are not told what he said to God, but I'm convinced it was an ancient Hebrew word pronounced something like *"Heeelp!"* Have you ever experienced a similar situation in which you were put on the spot and suddenly gripped with fear, without any time or opportunity to engage in a long, deeply meaningful prayer?

While on a trip to India, I was picked up at the airport and taken by taxi to my hotel. It was dark and the streets were filled with speeding cars, horns blaring. It seems that very few driving rules are enforced there; people just let you know where they are by blowing their horns. We were zipping along a road when, suddenly, we pulled up behind a slow-moving car. The taxi driver laid on his horn but to no avail. He decided to pass the car and, just as he pulled out, we saw a truck coming toward us. I thought to myself, *My driver will slow down and pull back in behind the car.* But instead, he floored the gas pedal. We shot forward and, at the last possible moment before impact (the oncoming vehicle wasn't slowing down either), we zipped in front of the other car and barely missed the oncoming truck! In those rapid-fire moments, there was only time for a quick prayer to the Father.

Recently, a friend who is a security police officer for a nearby mall told of a harrowing experience. He was in his police car on the third level of the parking deck when the dispatcher sent out an alarm. At that moment, larceny was taking place in one of the stores. Suddenly, a man matching the thief's description came running out from the store, carrying several items.

My friend anxiously jumped out of the car and shouted, "Halt!" The fleeing suspect then changed directions and proceeded to run even faster. The security officer began pursuing the man and was inches behind him when they reached the edge of the third level parking deck. The suspect then jumped over the railing. The guard knew that there was a mound of grass five feet below the deck, so he jumped, too. However, he had miscalculated exactly where he was, and fell all the way to the ground—twenty-two feet below! He broke a leg but told me that, as he was falling, he thought his life could very well be over. He recalled instantly attending a "short prayer meeting"! Afterward, he was praising the Lord for only a broken leg.

You may have been in a situation where the phone has rung, the boss has summoned, the teacher has called, the doctor's office has reported—you are immediately filled with fear, and you don't have much time to pray. What we observe in the life of Nehemiah is that sort of unexpected panic that comes with a lack of control. We are allowed to see him as the genuine person that he is: terrified, surprised, and breathing a quick prayer to the God of heaven. A short prayer is best preceded by consistent praying. The key to effective praying before God is not *length* but *loyalty*. When you walk with God moment by moment, every day of every week, you do not have to say very much in those emergency moments of life.

A SUBMISSIVE APPEAL

I said to the king, "If it please the king, and if your servant has found favor before you, send me to Judah, to the city of my fathers' tombs, that I may rebuild it" (Nehemiah 2:5).

This is gracious tact on Nehemiah's part. He did not say, "I'm glad you asked, O King. God has a job for me, so I want a leave of absence. I'll be back when God's finished with me in Jerusalem. Have you got a problem with that?" No, Nehemiah is willing to allow God to move through the heart of the king to grant him permission to go.

A SUBTLE INFLUENCE

Then the king said to me, the queen sitting beside him, "How long will your journey be, and when will you return?" So it pleased the king to send me, and I gave him a definite time (Nehemiah 2:6).

Why the rather obvious and somewhat awkward insertion that the queen was sitting by the king? Because the queen did *not* usually sit beside the king during his business day. Do you remember how Queen Esther dared to even come into the king's presence without an invitation? *(Esther 4:16)*. The clear implication, recorded in Nehemiah's memoirs, is that the queen was not only present but seated beside the king during "business hours." She may very well have had an influence over the king while Nehemiah presented his request.

There are some who have pointed out that if this is the Artaxerxes we think it is chronologically, then the queen was not Artaxerxes' wife. In addition, it is important to note that "queen" was also used for the queen mother. The queen mother (or stepmother, in this case) would have been none other than *Esther* herself! Perhaps this is why the king was so favorable to Nehemiah's bold and comprehensive request—a request that would be costly to the kingdom—but a request, nonetheless, that would aid the people of his stepmother Esther.

A SOLID PLAN

Evidently, Nehemiah has been doing much more than praying; he has been planning, as well. Having gathered his wits about him, he now launches into a presentation of a very solid plan of action:

> *And I said to the king, "If it please the king, let letters be given me for the governors of the provinces beyond the River, that they may allow me to pass through until I come to Judah, and a letter to Asaph the keeper of the king's forest, that he may give me timber to make beams for the gates of the fortress which is by the temple, for the wall of the city and for the house to which I will go"* (Nehemiah 2:7–8).

NECESSITIES ANTICIPATED BY NEHEMIAH

- Written permission from the king for traveling from Susa to Jerusalem
- Supplies for rebuilding the city

Nehemiah's encounter is reminiscent of a girl going to her father and asking for money to buy a new skirt. When he agrees, she says, "Well, if I get a new skirt, I'll need something to wear with it." And before you know it, she has a top, shoes, belt, earrings, and a purse.

If you think that Nehemiah just keeps going on and on here, you are absolutely right. By the time he has finished laying out all his requests, he has asked the king not only for permission to send letters demanding cooperation from local governments around Jerusalem but also for permission to requisition from the *king's own royal forests* all the lumber they will need to rebuild the gates! I can only imagine Asaph scratching his head in bewilderment as he reads the letter from the king commanding him to give Nehemiah anything he needs. This would be tantamount to the mayor and the town council not only agreeing to a new church's expansion plans but voting to finance the entire project. When Nehemiah walked into the king's presence that day, he was a cupbearer; when he walked out, he was the newly appointed leader of a construction project that would ultimately restore the city of Jerusalem to the people of God—a project paid for by King Artaxerxes.

ENTER THE REAL MCCOY

As observed in the life of Nehemiah, a real McCoy of authentic, genuine faith is revealed as he lives by two important principles:

1. **Realize that God's delays are not necessarily denials.**

   "O LORD, I beseech You, may Your ear be attentive to the prayer of Your servant and the prayer of Your servants who delight to revere Your name, and make Your servant successful today . . ." (Nehemiah 1:11).

It is interesting that for four months, God did not seem to do anything on any given day in answer to Nehemiah's plea. But now we begin to realize that God was actually in the process of doing something *in* Nehemiah before He would ever do anything *through* Nehemiah. The genuine believer is struck by the fact that God is as much interested in doing something in him as He is in doing something through him. When it seemed that nothing was happening, something actually was. God was not just preparing Jerusalem for Nehemiah—He was preparing Nehemiah for Jerusalem.

2. Refuse to accept credit for the accomplished work of God.

> *And the king granted them* [my requests] *to me because the good hand of my God was on me* (Nehemiah 2:8*b*).

Nehemiah recognized that what just happened was accomplished by God. It was not because Nehemiah was smart but because God was sovereign. It was not because Nehemiah was great but because God was gracious.

Donald K. Campbell, in his book *Nehemiah: Man in Charge*, quoted G. Gordon Liddy after he was released from prison for his involvement in the Watergate scandal. Liddy boasted, "I have found within myself all I need and all I ever will need. I am a man of great faith, but my faith is in George Gordon Liddy, and I have never failed me." This is an interesting perspective, having just been released from prison!

Nehemiah has just been released from the king's palace—with royal permission and with all the financial backing necessary to rebuild Jerusalem's walls. He was humble enough to recognize that, in spite of his planning, success was granted because of God's good hand.

> *Then I came to the governors of the provinces beyond the River and gave them the king's letters. Now the king had sent with me officers of the army and horsemen. When Sanballat the Horonite and Tobiah the Ammonite official heard about it, it was very displeasing to them that someone had come to seek the welfare of the sons of Israel* (Nehemiah 2:9–10).

Did you notice Nehemiah's self-description in these verses? He did not say "the cupbearer of the king has come" or "the leader chosen by God has come" but simply "*someone* had come," which could be rendered "a man had come." A genuine, authentic, down-to-earth, real believer never gets caught up with what he or she has done—or will do—for the Lord.

Charles Swindoll quotes in *The Tale of the Tardy Oxcart* that Samuel Logan Brengle, a great leader in the work of God several generations ago, said it best when he wrote:

The ax cannot boast of the trees it has cut down. It could do nothing but for the woodsman. He made it. He sharpened it. He uses it. The moment the woodsman throws the ax aside, it becomes only old iron. Oh, that I may never lose sight of this.

Do you want to be a *real* McCoy? Do you want to avoid the imitations, the knockoffs of spirituality that abound today in the religious world? Allow yourself to be an instrument in the hands of God for His purposes and for His glory. Then, when He accomplishes something through you, don't ever forget that He was the One who did it.

Someone has come to seek the welfare of the sons of Israel—just a man, an ordinary someone. Yet, upon closer inspection, we have discovered that he was actually a genuine, authentic man who was sometimes filled with fear and sometimes moved by faith.

Nehemiah may have considered himself only a *someone*, but in the final analysis, he was the *real* McCoy.

So I came to Jerusalem and was there three days. ¹²And I arose in the night, I and a few men with me. I did not tell anyone what my God was putting into my mind to do for Jerusalem and there was no animal with me except the animal on which I was riding. ¹³So I went out at night by the Valley Gate in the direction of the Dragon's Well and on to the Refuse Gate, inspecting the walls of Jerusalem which were broken down and its gates which were consumed by fire. ¹⁴Then I passed on to the Fountain Gate and the King's Pool, but there was no place for my mount to pass. ¹⁵So I went up at night by the ravine and inspected the wall. Then I entered the Valley Gate again and returned. ¹⁶The officials did not know where I had gone or what I had done; nor had I as yet told the Jews, the priests, the nobles, the officials or the rest who did the work. ¹⁷Then I said to them, "You see the bad situation we are in, that Jerusalem is desolate and its gates burned by fire. Come, let us rebuild the wall of Jerusalem so that we will no longer be a reproach." ¹⁸I told them how the hand of my God had been favorable to me also about the king's words which he had spoken to me. Then they said, "Let us arise and build." So they put their hands to the good work. ¹⁹But when Sanballat the Horonite and Tobiah the Ammonite official, and Geshem the Arab heard it, they mocked us and despised us and said, "What is this thing you are doing? Are you rebelling against the king?" ²⁰So I answered them and said to them, "The God of heaven will give us success; therefore we His servants will arise and build, but you have no portion, right, or memorial in Jerusalem."

—Nehemiah 2:11–20

CHAPTER FIVE

BLOOD, SWEAT, AND TEARS

Nehemiah 2:11–20

O n May 10, 1940, Winston Churchill was elected Prime Minister of England. Shortly afterward, it would be his responsibility to unite his country when the fury of the Third Reich and the wrath of Adolph Hitler was directed toward England. But under Churchill's leadership, the Brits would not be cowed. Even during the darkest days of World War II, as Hitler's bombers pummeled English cities during the Blitz, Churchill's voice could be heard on the radio, broadcasting his stubborn refusal to yield, while rallying the British people to continue their resistance.

In one particular series of speeches, as quoted from James Montgomery Boice's book *Nehemiah, Learning to Lead* and Microsoft Encarta's *Churchill, Sir Winston Leonard Spencer*, Churchill declared:

> "Even though large tracts of Europe and many old and famous States have fallen or may fall into the grip of the Gestapo and all the odious apparatus of Nazi rule, we shall not flag or fail. We shall go on to the end, we shall fight in France, we shall fight on the seas and oceans, we shall fight with growing confidence and growing strength in the air, we shall defend our island, whatever the cost may be, we shall fight on the beaches, we shall fight on the landing grounds,

we shall fight in the fields and in the streets, we shall fight in the hills; we shall never surrender, and even if, which I do not for a moment believe, this island or a large part of it were subjugated and starving, then our Empire beyond the seas, armed and guarded by the British Fleet, would carry on the struggle, until, in God's good time, the New World, with all its power and might, steps forth to the rescue and the liberation of the Old . . . I have nothing to offer you but blood, toil, tears, and sweat . . . Let us therefore brace ourselves to our duties, and so bear ourselves that if the British Empire and its Commonwealth last for a thousand years, men will still say, 'This was their finest hour.' "

In the same vein, as we study chapter two of Nehemiah, we find him approaching his finest hour. So far, the battle has been invisible. Nehemiah has agonized with God for four months and has seen the miracle of the king's heart turned in his favor. Now, however, the battle becomes visible—as real as German bombs. It will no longer be waged in the prayer closet; it will be a battle out in the open where everyone can see and hear. Nehemiah's message will be similar to Churchill's, though given 2,100 years earlier. He will refuse to surrender to the enemy; he will promise his people final victory . . . and in the days ahead, he will also ask from them their blood, sweat, and tears. Together they will discover the painful, yet deepening, maturing truth that there is no such thing as *opportunity* without *opposition*.

OPPORTUNITY
Don't Just Do Something . . . *Stand There!*

Then I came to the governors of the provinces beyond the river and gave them the king's letters. Now the king had sent with me officers of the army and horsemen. When Sanballat the Horonite and Tobiah the Ammonite official heard about it, it was very displeasing to them that someone had come to seek the welfare of the sons of Israel. So I came to Jerusalem and was there three days. And I arose in the night, I and a few men with me. I did not tell anyone what my God was putting into my mind to do for Jerusalem and there was no animal with me except the animal on which I was riding (Nehemiah 2:9–12).

This is not exactly what you would expect to read. Nehemiah has the permission of the king; he has the financing he needs for the work, but for three days he has not told anyone in Jerusalem why he has even come. I would have expected Nehemiah to set up a trailer on the site, unload his gear, unpack his tools, hire the bricklayers, roll in the heavy equipment, interview the subcontractors, and have a backhoe start digging the footings. "Let's build some walls here!"

Maybe you're tempted to ask, "What's the hold-up, Nehemiah? You're losing time, man! Get going!" Have you ever felt impatient over a building project? When will it begin? How long will it take? Then once the process starts, you wonder if it will ever be completed! Even with today's modern mechanical wonders, we still think the building process is much too long. But can you imagine being an Israelite? They have actually been waiting, in effect, for more than a hundred years. I fear that we would give up if we had to wait that long. The truth is the Israelites *had* given up hope. They had grown so accustomed to their history of failure and defeat, and they could no longer even conceive of anyone trying to build their walls again. But here he is—the man with the plan, the permission, and the power to make it happen. Yet he's not even announcing his arrival. Had I been Nehemiah, I would have bounded into town shouting the news, "The king is on our side and is supplying our building needs. We're going to build these walls again!" But an announcement like that would have been a terrible mistake.

Wisdom Waits

I did not tell anyone what my God was putting into my mind to do for Jerusalem (Nehemiah 2:12).

This man arrived in town and for three days he said nothing. But this doesn't mean that Nehemiah was not doing anything. It was three days of waiting and, no doubt, three days of praying. He probably spent three days talking to the locals about their city and, perhaps, meeting the city officials. I am quite sure that Nehemiah was also taking inventory of their spiritual condition, along with the condition of their walls.

Wisdom Investigates

Then, without any explanation to us readers, he gets up late one night and, with a few of his armed escorts, takes a closer look at the conditions:

> *So I went out at night by the Valley Gate in the direction of the Dragon's Well and on to the Refuse Gate, inspecting the walls of Jerusalem which were broken down and its gates which were consumed by fire. Then I passed on to the Fountain Gate and the King's Pool, but there was no place for my mount to pass. So I went up at night by the ravine and inspected the wall. Then I entered the Valley Gate again and returned. The officials did not know where I had gone or what I had done; nor had I as yet told the Jews, the priests, the nobles, the officials or the rest who did the work* (Nehemiah 2:13–16).

This is Nehemiah's midnight ride. Even today, those who are involved in leadership are often awake while others sleep. I can assure you that the moment you sign on to serve others and the moment you accept the burden of rebuilding your broken world, you will have many sleepless nights. That is what Oswald Sanders called "the penalty of leadership."

The city sleeps while a burdened man inspects the damage. Verse 13 tells us that he *inspected* the walls. That is a Hebrew verb which can be translated "to carefully observe." It is a verb that is used in the medical profession to describe the probing of a wound to determine not only the damage but also the action needed for healing to take place. Now, if we had a map of Jerusalem, we would notice from the gates that Nehemiah has just mentioned that he was actually touring the southern portion of the broken-down city. He didn't see the whole city wall, but he saw enough to formulate his plan.

Between verses 16 and 17, more time elapses. We are not sure how much time, but perhaps it was just enough to announce a very important meeting.

Don't Just Stand There . . . *Do Something!*

Having gathered the people of Jerusalem—the priests, the nobles, and the officials—Nehemiah now announces his intentions:

Then I said to them, "You see the bad situation we are in, that Jerusalem is desolate and its gates burned by fire. Come, let us rebuild the wall of Jerusalem so that we will no longer be a reproach." I told them how the hand of my God had been favorable to me and also about the king's words which he had spoken to me. Then they said, "Let us arise and build." So they put their hands to the good work (Nehemiah 2:17–18).

Now if you're like me, perhaps you are a little surprised that after such a short speech the text says the people responded by saying, *"Let us arise and build."* At first glance—or even two or three closer looks—verses 17 and 18 don't seem to be enough of a motivational speech from Nehemiah to make any person be willing to risk his life. It certainly wasn't enough to move people to attempt something so terribly difficult that they hadn't been able to do for these many years.

Key Components in Rallying Helpers

Nehemiah has several key features in his speech which motivated the people to the very core of their beings. There are volumes in his words.

1. An honest attitude

Then I said to them, "You see the bad situation we are in, that Jerusalem is desolate and its gates burned by fire" (Nehemiah 2:17a).

Nehemiah's honesty is refreshing. He doesn't sugar-coat the problem. He does not start by saying, "I've seen the walls, and it's not all that bad." That's what you call an optimist—a person who takes a favorable view of everything. But that's better than being a pessimist, isn't it? Someone described a pessimist as one who is seasick during the entire voyage of life.

Charles Swindoll tells this story:

A farmer who was continually optimistic had a neighbor who was just the opposite. Grim and gloomy, his neighbor faced each new day with a frown. The optimistic farmer would see the sun coming up and shout over the roar of the tractor,

"Look at that beautiful sun and clear sky!" With a frown, the negative neighbor would reply, "Yeah, it'll probably scorch the crops."

When clouds gathered and much-needed rain started to fall, the positive farmer would smile across the fence, "Ain't this great—God is giving our corn a drink today!" Again, a negative response, "Uh-huh, but if it don't stop before long, it'll flood and wash everything away."

One day, the optimist decided to try to trump his neighbor's pessimism. He bought the smartest, most expensive bird dog he could find and trained him to do things no other dog on earth could do—impossible, even miraculous, feats that would amaze and delight anyone. He invited the pessimist to go duck hunting, and they sat in the duck blind. The ducks flew over. Both men fired and several ducks fell into the water. "Go get 'em!" ordered the owner to his dog.

The dog leapt out of the boat, ran on the water to where the ducks were floating, gathered them in his mouth, and ran back to the boat and jumped in. "Well, what do you think of that?" the optimist asked.

Unsmiling, the pessimist answered, "*Hah!* . . . can't swim, can he?"

Each of us would probably say we're not an optimist or a pessimist but a *realist*. Frankly, we would all like to think that we've found a balance between the two extremes.

Well, Nehemiah had. You could call him a true, genuine, undeniable realist. He did not overlook problems, nor was he overwhelmed by them. He immediately earned respect by verbalizing his understanding of the people's painful condition. Notice his refusal to mince words: "It's a bad situation . . . pretty desolate . . . the gates are burned by fire."

2. A humble identification

> ***Then I said to them, "You see the bad situation we are in . . .
> Come, let us rebuild the wall of Jerusalem so that we will no
> longer be a reproach"*** (Nehemiah 2:17).

He didn't say, "Man, are you in a bad situation! What *you* need to do
is to rebuild the wall of Jerusalem so that *you* will no longer be a reproach."
No, he used *we* and *us*. If you want to discourage someone whose life is in
ruins, just say, "Man, are you a mess; you really ought to do something about
that." It will work every time. On the other hand, if you want to encourage
them, begin by saying, "This is a mess. How can we get out of this together?"

3. An honorable invitation

Nehemiah didn't approach the people saying, "Listen, let's build a wall
so we'll have a nice enclosure" or "Let's build a wall around our city so we
can sleep at night without fear of invaders" or "Let's build a wall so we can
be a walled city like the others." All of these things would be true—just not
honorable. Nehemiah invites the people to **rebuild the wall of Jerusalem so
that we will no longer be a reproach** (Nehemiah 2:17).

The word translated *reproach* means to speak down to someone or to
speak ill of their character.

He said, "Hey, guys, let's rebuild the wall so we, the people of God, will
be so representative of Him that people around us can't speak poorly of our
character or disparage the character of God." This motivated the people to
action! What motivates you?

There are two basic types of motivation in life: *extrinsic* and *intrinsic*.

The father says to his son, "I want you to go out and mow the grass."

"Why?"

"Because it looks terrible."

The son doesn't budge; he's not motivated by how terrible the yard looks.

"Listen," his father adds, "go out there and cut the grass because there are
wild animals moving into our jungle and it's no longer safe outside!"

The son rather likes wild animals, yet remains totally unmoved.

Finally, in desperation, the father says, "Son, I'll pay you if you'll go out
there and cut the grass."

Zooom! The boy is out the door in a flash to get the mower. He simply
had to be motivated by something "outside" himself to perform the task.

That is extrinsic motivation.

Intrinsic motivation is when you do something because of an internal desire or passion. You will not get an immediate reward for performing it, but you will find fulfillment in knowing that you did the right thing. The highest intrinsic motivation is the desire to bring glory and honor to the reputation of God, whom you represent on earth. So you refuse to lie and cheat; you choose to share and show kindness; you practice patience and peace—all because you want your life to reflect credit on the Lord.

Will your boss ever pay you for honesty? Will your classmates ever praise you for purity? Will an award ever be given to you for character? Most likely the answer to the above questions is no. However, you try to live out those characteristics because you don't want to be the cause of reproach before people, which ultimately brings reproach to your God. You are, therefore, *intrinsically* motivated to honor God. That is the type of motivation that Nehemiah used to inspire a discouraged nation.

4. A hope-filled testimony

> *I told them how the hand of my God had been favorable to me, and also about the king's words which he had spoken to me* (Nehemiah 2:18*a*).

Can you imagine how the people must have hung on every word? "God is here with us," Nehemiah declares. "God has prepared the way. He has turned the heart of the king. He has supplied our financial need. He has not forgotten you, dear friends. He has not forgotten His holy city."

For those of you who work in a position where you are ministering to other people—whether teaching a class, caring for children, discipling believers, greeting visitors, praying, working as a vocational missionary, or serving in any capacity of ministry—you have probably discovered by now that one of the most discouraging things is that you are never finished. Because of that, you are often left wondering if God is really accomplishing anything through your efforts and your prayers.

I recently received a letter which was written by a young lady who left our church to attend college in another state. While her remarks were written to me, it is obvious that she speaks of our church at large. Our church has, together as a body, become the kind of church that this college freshman now remembers with fond memories. She wrote:

> One thing that I really appreciated is how our church, from the time of meeting in a middle school building and all the way to completing our current building, focused on the greatness of God.

I have read that a dozen times . . . what wonderful encouragement to be viewed as having a focus on the greatness of our God! She continued:

> Another thing was how missions stayed a priority in our church. No matter how we may have struggled financially in the past, and especially in raising money for our new land and building, we never stopped giving to missionaries. I think that is so neat.
>
> I know I will never be able to express all my gratitude to you about what an impact the church has in my life, but I wanted you to know that it's because of this church that I am a believer today and am now headed toward full-time missions in the future.

This young lady had been attending our church since she was eleven years old; there are people in our church who were once her Sunday school teachers. No doubt, her teachers once wondered if God was accomplishing anything in the lives of these pre-teen girls. How encouraging to hear words that reveal God has been at work.

It must have been equally encouraging to the people of Jerusalem to hear a man say, "I know you've lived for years surrounded by these broken-down walls. You don't think God is even noticing anymore. But I want you to know that God has been favorable to me. He has been at work in my life, and He is at work even now among you." No wonder they all shouted in unison:

> **"Let us arise and build." So they put their hands to the good work** (Nehemiah 2:18*b*).

OPPOSITION

This would be a wonderful place for the Book of Nehemiah to end—but it doesn't. Instead, just as eagerly as the people *put their hands to the good work*, the enemy put his hand to stopping their work.

Three Enemies of the Cause

But when Sanballat the Horonite and Tobiah the Ammonite official and Geshem the Arab heard it, they mocked us and despised us and said, "What is this thing you are doing? Are you rebelling against the king?" (Nehemiah 2:19).

1. Sanballat was the governor of Samaria.

2. Tobiah ruled the kingdom of Ammon.

3. Geshem and his sons ruled the Arab nations.

These men were powerful enemies of God and of His people.

When you decide to build anything for the glory of God—whether a godly home, a pure mind, honest character, or numerous other things—anything and anyone who opposes God will oppose you. There is no opportunity from heaven without opposition from hell. If you think that walking with Christ is a path strewn with flowers, think again. Jesus Christ warned His disciples that the object which would grace their necks would not be a garland but a cross:

> *Then Jesus said to His disciples, "If anyone wishes to come after Me, he must deny himself, and take up his cross and follow Me"* (Matthew 16:24).

Christianity is not always blessings, sweetness, and triumph. Sometimes it is blood, sweat, and tears. And more often than not, the enemies of the cross seem to outnumber its friends.

Two Forms of Opposition

The enemies of Nehemiah opposed the work in two strategic ways:

1. Public ridicule

[T]*hey mocked us and despised us* (Nehemiah 2:19*b*).

2. Personal intimidation

"What is this thing you are doing?" (Nehemiah 2:19*c*).

Public ridicule was intended to produce personal embarrassment. Intimidation was intended to produce fear. These two forms of opposition—embarrassment and fear—have worked wonders in keeping Christians from doing or saying anything for God. Perhaps it would work against Nehemiah.

Nehemiah's Six-Part Response

So I answered them and said to them, "The God of heaven will give us success; therefore we His servants will arise and build, but you have no portion, right, or memorial in Jerusalem" (Nehemiah 2:20).

Nehemiah responds to the opposition by saying six significant things:

1. This is God's work.
2. We are God's servants.
3. This work will be accomplished by God's power.
4. You have no portion here, i.e., no property inside the city.
5. You have no right—no claim of authority over Jerusalem. It could also imply that they have no right to require taxes or tribute from the citizens of Jerusalem.
6. You have no memorial. This is a religious implication that could be amplified to read, "You have no place of worship within Jerusalem's community of believers."

His courage was fortified by the power of God Almighty. The enemies' intimidation and ridicule did not discourage the work. What about the "good work" we have been given to do? Are we moving forward, or are we discouraged and defeated by ridicule and intimidation?

How to Avoid the Danger of Discouragement

First, understand that God's will is not always *easy*, but it is always *possible* by His might.

"[W]ith God, all things are possible" (Matthew 19:26*b*).

Second, rest in the fact that God will never command you to do anything without providing the strength and the means to accomplish it.

> [F]*or it is God who is at work in you, both to will and to work for His good pleasure* (Philippians 2:13).

The following from the Jack Handey book *Fuzzy Memories* was quoted in *Fresh Illustrations for Preaching and Teaching*:

> There used to be this bully who would demand my lunch money every day at school. Since I was smaller than he was, I would give it to him. Then I decided to fight back. I started taking karate lessons. But then the karate instructor told me I owed him five dollars a lesson. So I just went back to paying the bully. Too many people feel it is easier just to pay the bully than it is to learn how to defeat him.

God never commands you to live for His glory without helping you to overcome the obstacles you will face. Whether it's loving your spouse, witnessing to friends and relatives, or remaining pure on a college campus, you will be enabled by Christ if you obey Him:

> *I can do all things through Him who strengthens me* (Philippians 4:13).

Imagine what Nehemiah must have thought as he toured the city that night. There were huge stones lying on the ground, even piled up at places. There was a century of weeds and underbrush, as well as the rotten wood of former gates crumbled to the ground. Had you or I been Nehemiah, we probably would have taken the first camel back to Persia. But he *knew* that God's good hand was upon him, strengthening him for this monumental task.

Third, rejoice in the principle that opposition only means opportunity is close at hand. Since there is never opportunity without opposition, you learn to welcome not only the opportunity but the obstacle as well. Do you remember a difficult experience where you were tempted to quit but you kept on going? By refusing to surrender, you—like the British nation under the leadership of Churchill—can say that it was your finest hour.

Paul encourages us as we follow the leadership of Christ to never surrender or throw in the towel. He challenged the Corinthians and every Christian to be *steadfast, immovable, always abounding in the work of the Lord, knowing that your toil is not in vain in the Lord* (1 Corinthians 15:58).

What a great promise: your toil is not in vain. Endurance that demands blood, sweat, and tears *will* be rewarded one day. In the meantime, by the Lord's empowering, you can dare to say, "Let us arise and build!"

Then Eliashib the high priest arose with his brothers the priests and built the Sheep Gate; they consecrated it and hung its doors. They consecrated the wall to the Tower of the Hundred and the Tower of Hananel. ²Next to him the men of Jericho built, and next to them Zaccur the son of Imri built. ³Now the sons of Hassenaah built the Fish Gate; they laid its beams and hung its doors with its bolts and bars. ⁴Next to them Meremoth the son of Uriah the son of Hakkoz made repairs. And next to him Meshullam the son of Berechiah the son of Meshezabel made repairs. And next to him Zadok the son of Baana also made repairs. ⁵Moreover, next to him the Tekoites made repairs, but their nobles did not support the work of their masters. ⁶Joiada the son of Paseah and Meshullam the son of Besodeiah repaired the Old Gate; they laid its beams and hung its doors with its bolts and its bars. ⁷Next to them Melatiah the Gibeonite and Jadon the Meronothite, the men of Gibeon and of Mizpah, also made repairs for the official seat of the governor of the province beyond the River. ⁸Next to him Uzziel the son of Harhaiah of the goldsmiths made repairs. And next to him Hananiah, one of the perfumers, made repairs, and they restored Jerusalem as far as the Broad Wall.

—Nehemiah 3:1–8

CHAPTER SIX

CONSTRUCTION SITES AND CHURCH CAFETERIAS

Nehemiah 3

For some time now, I have been collecting different articles related to the subject of following directions—something I'm not accustomed to doing. In fact, my family still laughs about the time many Christmases ago when I insisted I could put my daughter's tricycle together without consulting the directions. All went well . . . until the final step of attaching the seat. For some reason, it didn't seem to fit no matter how many different ways I turned it. Frustrated, I finally looked at the directions and discovered that the frame of the tricycle had been assembled upside down!

In an effort to break my former habit of not reading directions, I did read the ones found on a flat iron that was purchased by my older daughter for straightening hair. Some of them were painfully obvious: "Do not use while in the shower." Another warned, "Do not drop this into water." Still another: "Do not let heated surfaces touch your eyes." Here was the one I really found hard to imagine the company even putting into print: "Never use while sleeping." Now I remember why I had stopped reading directions in the first place!

Here are some other brilliant instructions:

- Tesco's Tiramisu dessert box – "Do not turn upside down." And where do you think this warning was written? On the bottom, of course.

- Marks & Spencer Bread Pudding – "Product will be hot after heating."

- Children's cough medicine – "Do not drive a car after taking this medication."

- Nytol Sleep Aid – "Warning: may cause drowsiness."

- Superman costume for children – "Wearing of this garment does not enable one to fly." Pity the child who learns the hard way.

This true story printed in the journal *Feathers* was told by John MacArthur:

> The "Chicken Gun," as NASA calls it, has been specifically built to launch a dead chicken at maximum velocity directly onto the windshields of airliners, military jets, and even the space shuttle. The idea is to test the strength of the windshield materials and construction by simulating the frequent incidents of collisions with airborne fowl.
>
> British engineers heard about the gun and wanted to use it to test the windshield of their newest high-speed train. The gun was sent, the testing site was arranged, and the gun was loaded with a dead chicken. When the gun was fired, the engineers stood in shocked silence as the chicken hurtled out of the barrel, smashed through the shatterproof windshield, blasted through the control console, broke the engineer's backrest in two, and embedded itself in the back wall of the cabin. The horrified British sent NASA the disastrous results of the experiment, explaining the design of the windshield, what they had done, and then asked for further suggestions. NASA responded with a one-liner: "Next time, thaw the chicken."

I think that most of us would agree, when it comes to testing windshields, taking medicine, or using new equipment, following the directions (silly as some of them may sound) is an important thing to do. This past week and on any given week, seventy or more churches throughout our land closed their doors and went out of business. While I am sure that there is a host of reasons behind that tragic statistic, I am convinced that, for the most part, those churches *failed to read the directions*.

While most people would follow the directions on how to use a new lawn mower, many Christians believe that a church somehow operates on its own—without any divine direction. Certainly any church at times has blasted a frozen chicken or two into the air. But the church that desires to honor God will never attempt to do it on its own—rather, it uses God's divine blueprint, the Bible.

BUILDING THE BODY

What is a church, anyway? The Greek word for church is *ekklesia*. It comes from the verb *kalew* which means "to call." The prefix further defines the word to mean "called out ones." What a wonderful definition.

The Church Is Called Out from the World

It is a separated group of people who have been redeemed by the grace of God. Like shipwrecked and drowning people in an ocean, we have been rescued on the lifeboat *Grace*. We have been rescued by the Gospel of Jesus Christ. But that is just the beginning. The Church is not just called out from the world.

The Church Is Commissioned to Go Back into the World

The "called out ones" band together and pool their resources and then go back to the site of the shipwreck and pull as many people into their boat as they possibly can. But how do you manage this band of people called the Church? How does it operate? Where are the directions? What do they say?

The set of blueprints is found in a first-century letter. In that letter you discover that the Church is not only called out of the world and commissioned to go back into the world—it has another function.

The Church Has Been Created to Act like a Living, Human Body

For the body is not one member, but many. If the foot says, "Because I am not a hand, I am not a part of the body," it is not for this reason any the less a part of the body. And if the ear says, "Because I am not an eye, I am not a part of the body," it is not for this reason any the less a part of the body. If the whole body were an eye, where would the hearing be? If the whole were hearing, where would the sense of smell be? But now God has placed the members, each one of them, in the body, just as He desired (1 Corinthians 12:14–18).

The manual on operating the Church looks more like an anatomy chart than an organizational chart. Every person has a role to play in the body. We have people who are designed to be the hands, feet, mouth, ears, and nose. Everyone operates according to the gift or gifts which God has given him, and then he becomes the gift of God to other parts of the body as a whole.

D.L. Moody, who over one hundred years ago founded a church, a school, a publishing house, and more, said,

A great many people have a false idea about the church. They have an idea that the church is a place to simply rest in . . . to get into a nicely cushioned pew, and contribute to the charities, listen to the minister, and do their share to keep the church out of bankruptcy. The idea of work for them—actual work in the church—never enters their minds.

That's an indicator that many church members are *not* reading the directions:

And He gave some as apostles, and some as prophets, and some as evangelists, and some as pastors and teachers, for the equipping of the saints for the work of service, to the building up of the body of Christ; until we all attain to the unity of the faith (Ephesians 4:11–13*a*).

"The unity of faith" is a key phrase to understand. What does it mean when it says we are attempting to *attain to the unity of the faith*? When the word *faith* is preceded by the article *the*, it is referring to a body of truth—doctrinal truth—that forms the foundation of our faith:

[T]he faith which was once for all handed down to the saints (Jude 1:3*b*).

The word of God kept on spreading; and the number of the disciples continued to increase greatly in Jerusalem, and a great many of the priests were becoming obedient to the faith (Acts 6:7).

Paul said of himself,

"He who once persecuted us [the Church] *is now preaching the faith which he once tried to destroy"* (Galatians 1:23).

Our unity is always built upon our body of truth, frequently called "the faith." Unity is not derived from everyone thinking alike, everyone liking the same kind of music, or everyone eating the same kind of food. Our unity is not based on personality, appearance, or social standing. Our unity is based on our collective commitment to *the faith*—the truth of Holy Scripture. Paul emphasized this when he wrote:

As a result, we are no longer to be children, tossed here and there by waves and carried about by every wind of doctrine, by the trickery of men, by craftiness in deceitful scheming; but speaking the truth in love, we are to grow up in all aspects into Him who is the head, even Christ, from whom the whole body, being fitted and held together by what every joint supplies, according to the proper working of each individual part, causes the growth of the body for the building up of itself in love (Ephesians 4:14–16).

BENEFITS OF "BODY" BUILDING

According to those spiritual directions, Paul tells us that two things will happen when the body (or the Church) grows like it should.

We Are Rescued from Spiritual Deception

When you build up the body of Christ *(Ephesians 4:12)* by attaining to the unity of the faith *(Ephesians 4:13)*, you are mature enough to keep from falling into spiritual deception *(Ephesians 4:14)*.

I have fun teasing and joking with my children. I remember telling my younger daughter something at the dinner table when she was five, then laughing along with the family because of the way she had been fooled.

I said, "Honey, it's okay, Daddy's just pulling your leg."

She immediately looked under the table at her legs and said, "No you're not, Daddy."

Upset at being fooled once, she was *not* going to be fooled again.

Part of growing up as a body of believers is that together we avoid the deception of false teachers. We stop believing everything we hear.

Body Building Not Only Rescues Us from Spiritual Deception but Also from Spiritual Disability

> *From whom the whole body, being fitted and held together by what every joint supplies,* [tendon and ligament and nerve and blood vessel] *according to the proper working of each individual part, causes the growth of the body for the building up of itself in love* (Ephesians 4:16).

You are not responsible to answer whether someone *else* is supplying their part for the functioning of the body. The key question for you is whether *you* are supplying your part to the building up of the body in love. When every joint of the body does its job, the body is not disabled—it's coordinated. That is true with a physical body and it's true with the spiritual body called the local church.

People who join a church and do not serve become like disabled, ineffective parts of a human body. In fact, if a person has a body part that doesn't function as it should, we call that person disabled or handicapped. When people attach themselves to the church and refuse to function, the church becomes disabled and handicapped in the ministry. On the other hand, when everyone rolls up their sleeves and humbly, lovingly serve one another, that church is actually protecting itself from spiritual deception and spiritual disability.

One Sunday a church's members met at a restaurant for lunch. One woman was carrying her bowl of soup to the table when she stumbled, tipped her bowl, slipped and fell in the puddle of soup. If we as believers were there using our gifts, the scene would have looked something like this:

- One who is a gifted pastor or shepherd would immediately form a line and guide people around the woman so they wouldn't slip on the spilled soup or trip over the woman.

- One with the gift of mercy would immediately go and sit down with the woman on the cafeteria floor and whisper, "I know how you must feel. Here, let me wipe some of this soup off your clothing."

- The gifted teacher would stand and say, "May I have your attention, please. This dear woman has fallen and spilled her soup. You could translate the word *spill* 'to tip out' or 'to tilt in an extreme direction.' There are three reasons why she spilled her soup—so get ready to take notes in order to prevent spilling your soup as well."

- One with the gift of giving is patiently waiting for the woman to be seated at her table . . . so he can give her his bowl of soup.

- The gifted exhorter, after the woman has been seated at a table, leads everyone in the cafeteria in a round of three cheers for the woman who was willing to get back up on her feet.

- The gifted servants arrive with a mop and pail to clean everything up and put the cafeteria back in order.

Finding your place in the church cafeteria is not really that difficult, but it doesn't just happen, either. It is born of a willingness to supply whatever you can provide. And you discover that when you do, just as Paul said, it *causes the growth of the body for the building up of itself in love* (Ephesians 4:16*b*).

Now, where in the Bible can we find an illustration of a group of people who are acting like the Church is supposed to act? Would you believe . . . **Nehemiah 3**?

LESSONS FROM AN OLD TESTAMENT CONSTRUCTION SITE

Nehemiah's plan was to rebuild and repair the wall in Jerusalem. His strategy could be summarized with the phrase "divide and conquer," for that is exactly what he will do. About forty names are given of those who headed the many task forces. Nehemiah has given key positions to people who will lead, organize, and encourage the others. It is obvious that Nehemiah has carefully *planned his work*. Now, he will carefully *work his plan*.

There are a number of lessons that Nehemiah provides to the New Testament church.

People Who Were Willing to Work Were Given the Opportunity

Whether priests or professionals, noble-born or common stock, single men or women—all are mentioned in the work. The same goes for professionals and politicians, native residents and outsiders, construction crews and artisans—all who were willing to work were given jobs to do. Some would repair the wall closest to their homes. Others were commuters who were sent to various locations. Some repaired existing walls while others started from scratch, using the blocks that had previously broken down. Some of the workers labored on the different gates, with their massive hinges and bolts, while others picked up rubble and carted trash away.

It is interesting that the very first group of workers Nehemiah listed in his memoirs were people led by the high priest:

> **Then Eliashib the high priest arose with his brothers the priests and built the Sheep Gate; they consecrated it and hung its doors. They consecrated the wall to the Tower of the Hundred and the Tower of Hananel** (Nehemiah 3:1).

These towers were on the westward side of the Sheep Gate. This was the place where sacrificial lambs and sheep would enter to be offered for the sins of the people. Since the priests performed the atoning services, this would be a significant wall to them—in fact, they may have considered it holy ground. Therefore, we can see the significance of Nehemiah assigning them to work in this particular location. They could not possibly have known that approximately four hundred years later, Jesus Christ Himself, the Lamb of God, would walk through that reconstructed gate to pray in a nearby garden called Gethsemane. Later, He was undoubtedly brought back through that same gate by the soldiers who arrested Him and took Him before the Sanhedrin. He was, indeed, the final Lamb led to the slaughter *(Isaiah 53:7)*.

Priests do not typically work with stones and hammers. However, this was not a typical situation, and they gladly set an example for the rest of the people.

People Who Did Not Necessarily Know How to Do the Work but They Were Willing to Learn

Next to him Uzziel the son of Harhaiah of the goldsmiths made repairs. And next to him Hananiah, one of the perfumers, made repairs, and they restored Jerusalem as far as the Broad Wall. Next to them Rephaiah the son of Hur, the official of half the district of Jerusalem, made repairs (Nehemiah 3:8–9).

Imagine a politician, a goldsmith, and a perfume maker *laying bricks!* What did they know about building walls and slapping on mortar? It didn't matter. Evidently, Nehemiah provided them with additional workers who could show them how. The person who says he cannot work because he does not know how should learn a lesson from a perfume maker who has exchanged sweet-smelling vials of delicately scented liquid for a pile of rocks and a trowel.

People Who Were Able to Do More Work than Others

In a number of verses (11, 19, 21, 24, 27, 30), you have an interesting phrase repeated: *they repaired another section.* In other words, these people did the job they were asked to do, and then they did more. What a tremendous testimony of people who went the extra mile!

People Who Were Willing to Work in More Difficult Places than Others

Malchijah the son of Rechab, the official of the district of Beth-haccherem repaired the Refuse Gate (Nehemiah 3:14a).

That name Refuse Gate can be translated *Dung* Gate. This was the gate through which all the garbage, manure, and refuse was taken. Here is a member of the royal caste willingly working in a filthy place where he could smell the stench from the Valley of Hinnom below.

Compare his working conditions with the location mentioned in the next verse:

> *Shallum the son of Col-hozeh, the official of the district of Mizpah, repaired the Fountain Gate. He built it, covered it and hung its doors with its bolts and its bars, and the wall of the Pool of Shelah at the king's garden as far as the steps that descend from the city of David* (Nehemiah 3:15).

In other words, you have one official who willingly works near the garbage dump and another official who gets to work by the pool near the king's flower gardens. This emphasizes again that some of the people were willing to work in more difficult places than others—*without complaining.*

People Who Were Willing to Work Harder than Others

> *After him Baruch the son of Zabbai zealously repaired another section, from the Angle to the doorway of the house of Eliashib the high priest* (Nehemiah 3:20).

This is the only person whose attitude or "spirit" is specifically mentioned. The Hebrew word translated *zealously* comes from a word that means "to burn or to glow." Just because you work willingly at a task does not necessarily mean you are working with a glow. Baruch represents those who work—and smile while they are at it. They show up at their posts with cheer and kind words. They are a pleasure to serve with and around. May the tribe of Baruch increase in the Church today.

People Who Were Able to Work Would Not

> *Moreover, next to him the Tekoites made repairs, but their nobles did not support the work of their masters* (Nehemiah 3:5).

We are not told why, but we are informed by Nehemiah that there were some who refused to help. The Tekoite nobles wouldn't work, but the common people would. It's not any different in the Church today. The tasks related to ministry are filled with ordinary people with a zeal for the Savior. Those who are "influential" in the world's eye tend to be occupied with more important things to do:

> [B]*ut God has chosen the foolish things of the world to shame the wise, and God has chosen the weak things of the world to shame the things which are strong and the base things of the world and the despised God has chosen* (1 Corinthians 1:27–28*a*).

People Who Worked with Their Hands Revealed the Condition of Their Hearts

If you skip ahead to **Nehemiah 4**, you discover a wonderful description of the workers. Oh, that these characteristics would be true of believers today:

> **So we built the wall and the whole wall was joined together to half its height, for the people had a mind to work** (Nehemiah 4:6).

A QUESTION YOU NEED TO ANSWER FOR YOURSELF

Churches are more like construction sites and cafeterias than palaces and winter resorts. It may not be glamorous work, but it is a place where God is honored and the work is never done in vain. In fact, the results will last forever because we are building people—and people last forever. The Apostle Peter reminds us that we all have received a special gift:

> [E]*mploy it in serving one another as good stewards of the manifold grace of God . . . whoever serves is to do so as one who is serving by the strength which God supplies; so that in all things God may be glorified through Jesus Christ* (1 Peter 4:10–11*b*).

The Lord has placed you at a "wall"; which of the seven characteristics describes your attitude and your effort? What does the work of your hands reveal about the condition of your heart?

Now it came about that when Sanballat heard that we were rebuilding the wall, he became furious and very angry and mocked the Jews. ²He spoke in the presence of his brothers and the wealthy men of Samaria and said, "What are these feeble Jews doing? Are they going to restore it for themselves? Can they offer sacrifices? Can they finish in a day? Can they revive the stones from the dusty rubble even the burned ones?" ³Now Tobiah the Ammonite was near him and he said, "Even what they are building—if a fox should jump on it, he would break their stone wall down!" ⁴Hear, O our God, how we are despised! Return their reproach on their own heads and give them up for plunder in a land of captivity. ⁵Do not forgive their iniquity and let not their sin be blotted out before You, for they have demoralized the builders. ⁶So we built the wall and the whole wall was joined together to half its height, for the people had a mind to work.

—Nehemiah 4:1–6

CHAPTER SEVEN

STICKS AND STONES MAY BREAK MY BONES

Nehemiah 4:1–6

In 1845, John Franklin left England to discover a northwest passageway—a seaway for ships that connected the Atlantic and Pacific Oceans through the Canadian Arctic. According to Kent Hughes' commentary on James, Franklin took 138 specially chosen men from the Royal Navy on this expedition. No one knew what lay ahead. In fact, they didn't even seem to be aware of the severe weather conditions that they would encounter in and around the North Pole. Nevertheless, they sailed off in two state-of-the-art ships. Each was equipped with an auxiliary steam engine and a huge storeroom that could hold a twelve-day supply of coal, should steam power ever be needed during the voyage.

As the ships sailed amidst imperial pomp and glory, the crew was confident in their quest. However, they had no idea that they were unprepared for what was ahead in the ice-filled waters off northern Canada. In fact, the only clothing they took with them was their uniforms, overcoats, and thin scarves which had been provided by Her Majesty's Royal Navy. Two months after their departure, a British whaler made contact with the two ships off the coast of Canada. That was the last time that the expedition was seen by Europeans.

Search parties would spend over 50 years retracing the voyage of the two Franklin ships in an effort to piece together some of the puzzle. It is believed that *Terror* and *Erebus* became trapped in ice off King William Island in

September 1846 and never sailed again. According to a note later found on that island, Franklin died there on June 11, 1847.

The most devastating fact was the discovery that upon sailing neither ship had stocked their coal supply but had turned their huge storerooms into lounges filled with 1,200 volume libraries, an organ, and even cupboard space filled with elegant place settings of china and silver for all the officers. One historian said that the Franklin expedition was prepared for weather conditions inside the Royal Navy officer's club, not the Arctic Ocean.

Yes, these men had been proudly confident in themselves and their fine ships, but pride and confidence were not the tools needed to overcome the great challenges of the Arctic Ocean. They discovered too late that they were unprepared and underdressed.

Jesus Christ said,

> *"If the world hates you, you know that it has hated Me before it hated you"* (John 15:18).

Are you prepared for *that?*

He also warned His disciples,

> *"They will make you outcasts . . . but an hour is coming for everyone who kills you to think that he is offering service to God"* (John 16:2).

Are you dressed for *that?*

Jesus said,

> *"Do you suppose I came to grant peace on earth? I tell you, no, but rather division; for from now on five members in one household will be divided . . . father against son and son against father, mother against daughter and daughter against mother"* (Luke 12:51–53a).

Another Gospel adds, *"[P]ersecution arises because of* [the presence of] *the word"* (Matthew 13:21). Will confidence comfort you in the midst of *that?*

Throughout His ministry on earth, our Lord was mocked by the religious leaders. The chief priests mocked Him, Herod mocked Him, and eventually the soldiers at Golgotha mocked Him. The early Church was ridiculed at Pentecost, and Jerusalem despised the apostles and accused them by saying, *"They are full of sweet wine"* (Acts 2:13). On the very day the Spirit descended, the apostles were accused of being drunk. As church history unfolded, *Hebrews 11* recorded that many believers endured cruel mocking and even martyrdom. Are you ready for *that*?

Paul wrote to Timothy, and to us as well, predicting that *all who desire to live godly in Christ Jesus will be persecuted* (2 Timothy 3:12).

Paul personally admitted:

> [We] *are roughly treated . . . we are reviled . . . we are perse-cuted . . . we are slandered . . . we have become as the scum of the world, the dregs of all things, even until now* (1 Corinthians 4:11–13).

Can *your* faith withstand that?

For one hundred years, the Jews had grown accustomed to broken-down walls. They had chosen the comfort of mediocrity rather than brave the icy storm of conquest. But now, a man has arrived with tools for building and supplies necessary for an expedition of faith. He has counted the cost and knows exactly what to expect. He has brought along plenty of "coal."

It is important to understand that during the time of the Old Testament, the city of Jerusalem was the center of God's earthly purpose. To restore the city would be a terrible blow to the enemies of God's purpose and His people. Less than a week after Nehemiah sailed into town, the cold winds of adversity began to howl. The enemy, the reviler, the slanderer, the hater of God and His people also arrived, silently and secretly. A battle is brewing; a war of great conflict is about to begin.

Behind all opposition to the work of God is the chief opponent of God. Anytime heaven advances, hell opposes. Anytime someone desires to so live to see God glorified and His Church enhanced, supported, supplied, and defended, they are bound to feel the frigid winds of calamity stinging their cheeks. Whether or not Nehemiah knew it, *the adversary* had moved his primary base of operations just outside the city of Jerusalem.

A CLOSER LOOK AT THE ENEMY

Before we observe the unfolding of the opposition against Nehemiah, let's take a closer look at the enemy himself.

He has a number of disguises, as well as and a number of names:

- **Satan** – refers to his role as the adversary of God and God's people *(Job 1)*

- **Lucifer** – his original name; refers to his aura of light *(Isaiah 14:12)*

- **the devil** *(Matthew 4:1)* – means accuser; he constantly accuses God in the presence of people, and people in the presence of God *(Job 1)*

- **Beelzebub** *(Matthew 12:27)* – "Lord of the Flies," or "Master of the Flies"; it refers to his masterminding of everything that is corrupt and filthy

- **the ruler of this world** *(John 12:31)* – references Satan's limited sphere of influence and authority over fallen mankind

- **the power of darkness** *(Luke 22:53)*

- **the prince of the power of the air** *(Ephesians 2:2)*

- **the father of lies** – a name that indicates he is the source and the originator of lying *(John 8:44)*; lying is his native tongue

- **the tempter** *(1 Thessalonians 3:5)*

- **the god of this world** – another name which indicates Satan's preeminence over sinful humanity and the world system *(2 Corinthians 4:4)*

- **the enemy** *(Matthew 13:39)*

- **murderer** *(John 8:44)*

- **the evil one** *(1 John 2:13)*

- **the old serpent** *(Revelation 12:9)* – in the first book of the Bible, he is introduced as the serpent; in the last book of the Bible, he is referred to as the old serpent

- **your adversary** *(1 Peter 5:8)*

- **the angel of light** – the warning Paul gave the church in Corinth, and I might add, our church today:

For such men are false apostles, deceitful workers, disguising them-selves as apostles of Christ. No wonder, for even Satan disguises himself as an angel of light. Therefore it is not surprising if his servants also disguise themselves as servants of righteousness, whose end will be according to their deeds (2 Corinthians 11:13–15).

Satan and his teachers hide behind the vocabulary of righteousness but, meanwhile, they are attempting to deceive, manipulate, and lead their followers into unrighteousness.

- **the great red dragon** *(Revelation 12:3)* – context reveals his desire to shed blood, his penchant for war, his lust for killing, and his power to intimidate and deceive

HOW DOES THE ENEMY OF GOD OPERATE?

With Destructive Purpose

Your adversary, the devil, prowls around like a roaring lion, seeking someone to devour (1 Peter 5:8).

The word *devour* could be translated "discredit or destroy." In other words, Satan is obsessed with destroying the worship of the one true, living God, whose throne he coveted and for which he fought. He failed and was cast to earth, and ever since he has attempted to rob God's throne of worship and glory. Any Christian or church that is dedicated to bringing worship and glory to God will be opposed by the enemy.

When you align your purpose in life to bring glory and honor to God, then that one who opposes the glory of God will most assuredly oppose you. Satan operates with destructive purpose.

With Remarkable Proficiency

He is intelligent, discerning, and cunning. His kingdom is connected through communication systems that would blow our minds. Nevertheless, in the course of taking a closer look at the enemy, do not forget several things:

- **His power is *limited*.** He is not omnipresent, omniscient, or omnipotent.
- **His influence is *delegated*.** He cannot do anything apart from our sovereign God's approval. What he intends for evil, God turns

around for good. The serpent is a puppet, and the strings are held by the hand of God.

- **His destruction is *guaranteed*.** Make no mistake—Satan knows what the end of the Bible says. Even though he knows his future fate, his hatred and anger move him against the throne of God while he still has time remaining.

- **His success is constantly *hindered*.** Not only can he not lift one finger against God, he also is limited in what he can accomplish against a believer.

The believer who dares, by faith, to mount an expedition into enemy territory for the advancement of the Gospel has been given the proper clothing. God did not prepare us for Arctic conditions by dispensing silk scarves. No, the disciple has been given the strong armor of the believer, and *Ephesians 6* describes for us every piece necessary to protect us against the great dragon's fire-breathing schemes.

With Enormous Patience

Our enemy is as patient as any fisherman who drops a lure into the pond and waits. This dragon (and his minions) drops lures into the ponds of our lives and waits for weeks, years and, sometimes, a lifetime, if necessary.

His lures are given different titles in the New Testament:

- **methods** – *Put on the full armor of God, so that you will be able to stand firm against the* **[methodias]** *of the devil* (Ephesians 6:11).

  The *methodias* which gives us our transliterated word "method" implies the craftiness of the devil.

- **schemes** – *[T]hat no advantage would be taken of us by Satan; for we are not ignorant of his* **schemes** (2 Corinthians 2:11).

  Schemes is a word that could be translated "designs." It actually refers to intellectual capacity. Satan brilliantly designs ingenious tricks and snares to entrap the Church and the believer, and he lays those traps with great care and patience.

In *Under His Wings*, author Patsy Clairmont portrayed this patient fisherman:

Fishing is a good way to understand Satan's agenda for us. I come from a long line of fishermen, the kind who won't let you move around in the boat lest you disturb the fish. Some of my family have been known to sit in a rickety rowboat 24 hours at a time. They sit and watch for activity in and on the water. When the action is right, they cast out, hoping to snag a whopper. When the fish takes the bait, he's reeled in and soon becomes dinner. In much the same way, Satan slips his rowboat into the waters of our lives. Then he waits for our moments of weakness, watches for unmet needs, and lurks in the murky, unsettled issues of our lives. He carefully checks his tackle box and selects just the right bait. When he thinks the time is ideal, he casts his line and waits for as long as necessary for us to take the bait. Then he reels us in. Unlike the fishermen I've known, Satan never throws any back. In fact, he seems to favor the little ones.

And to think that the great dragon has had two thousand years to hone his fishing skills. Rest assured, he cannot snag our souls, but he can reel in our song. He cannot destroy our destiny, but he can discredit our character, our witness, and our testimony. That is . . . *if we take the bait.*

A CLOSER LOOK AT THE LURE

Nowhere can you find a list of Satan's schemes and methods on such obvious display as in **Nehemiah 4**, **5**, and **6**. While *the adversary, the tempter, the deceiver, the angel of light, the great dragon* is never mentioned by name in these chapters, if you look closely enough, you will see the shadow of his scales; you will smell the fire from his nostrils, and you will almost hear the dip of his oars in the water as he glides toward Jerusalem.

When he arrives, Lucifer will design several lures and drop them one at a time into the pond of Nehemiah's life. The one he uses at the onset of his entrapment is one of his most successful lures in sidetracking believers. It is simply called the lure of *ridicule*. It first surfaces as outright anger, but later, it is disguised in a costume of politically charged questions:

Now it came about that when Sanballat heard that we were rebuilding the wall, he became furious and very angry and mocked the Jews. He spoke in the presence of his brothers and the wealthy men of Samaria (Nehemiah 4:1–2a).

UNMASKING THE QUESTIONS
Their Strength Was Doubted

"What are these feeble Jews doing?" (Nehemiah 4:2a).

"What are these weak (withered) miserable Jews doing?" Today we might say, "Who do they think they are?" Goliath asked that same question when little David, armed only with a shepherd's sling and five smooth stones, came running out to fight him. One stone for Goliath and four more, should he need them, for each of Goliath's four brothers. The Israelite army held their breath, thinking to themselves, *Goliath is too big to kill.* But as one author imagined, David ran toward Goliath thinking to himself, *He's too big to miss!* However, when Goliath saw David coming toward him, he mocked him: *He disdained him; for he was but a youth* (1 Samuel 17:42b).

Alan Redpath wrote, as quoted by Donald K. Campbell in his book *Nehemiah: Man in Charge*:

> The world judges everything by size, by headlines, by imposing plans, by vast advertisements; and it pours contempt upon the feeble little flock of the people of God. "You, with your feeble prayer meetings. You, with your silly little plan of getting people converted one by one. How can you possibly stand alongside our great economic programs in which a whole world can be revolutionized in a few years? You have no intellect; you are out of date; you have no money; you have no status. You feeble little lot!"

Have you ever been laughed at for your faith? Have you ever faced ridicule for your relationship with Christ? Do you lose heart at the sound of laughter?

Their Intelligence Was Doubted

Are they going to restore it for themselves? (Nehemiah 4:2b).

In other words, "Do they really understand what they're attempting to do? They don't have the foggiest idea about how to build a wall! Look over there—that man knows nothing of building structures; he's a perfume maker. The man on the pile of rubble over there makes jewelry—he's never built a wall! Look in the pit; they actually have women mixing the mortar. What do they know about that?"

Have you ever felt just a little foolish before the "wisdom" of the world? Have you ever wilted before the accusation of an intimidating professor, a wealthy relative, or a dignified acquaintance? Imagine how the workers must have felt under this barrage.

Their Faith Was Questioned

"Can they offer sacrifices?" (Nehemiah 4:2c).

Derek Kidner is probably right when he rewords this question for our understanding by saying, "Are these Jews going to pray their wall up? It's their only hope it will ever happen!" What a clever lure. "Hey, have you forgotten that the faith of your fathers wasn't good enough to *keep* these walls up? Their faith hasn't been able to *rebuild* these same walls over the last one hundred years. Do you think you have *greater faith* than they had? Do you think *your* sacrifices will help . . . who do you think *you* are?"

Their Organizational Skills Were Challenged

"Can they finish in a day?" (Nehemiah 4:2d).

It was like saying, "You're going to need to finish this project in one day because your 'game plan' will *not* last. You will never be able to endure the cold temperatures very long—you'll freeze to death. You haven't prepared for a long winter."

Their Ability Was Questioned

Can they revive the stones from the dusty rubble, even the burned ones? (Nehemiah 4:2e).

"They don't have the ability to resurrect a wall out of the midst of a century of rubble. It'll never work! They'll never make it!" Then Tobiah, who was standing nearby, added his cynical jab:

> *"Even what they are building—if a fox should jump on it,*
> *he would break their stone wall down!"* (Nehemiah 4:3).

Imagine serving God under such circumstances. The people of God were insulted, mocked, and ridiculed. The enemies of God had carefully, purposefully, and specifically attacked their strength, intelligence, faith, organizational skill, and ability.

In his book *Be Determined*, Warren Wiersbe wrote, "Some people, who can stand bravely when they are shot at, will collapse when they are laughed at."

Meanwhile, the cunning dragon stands by watching and waiting. He does the same thing today. Have you heard his accusations and insults?

"You don't have the *skill* to raise godly children."

"You don't have the *strength* to live for Christ."

"You don't have the *intelligence* to stand up to the wisdom of the world."

"You don't have the *faith* to finish anything for God."

"You don't have any *ability*! Who do you think you are anyway?"

Has the dragon dropped the lure of ridicule into the waters of your life recently? Then you probably know how powerful this lure was to the people who were following Nehemiah. Surely it would bring the work to a halt. Surely someone would say, "Nehemiah, they're right. We just might as well admit it. We don't know what we're doing. We are not wallbuilders! Why don't we stop the project now before we spend even more time and energy for nothing."

THREE WAYS NEHEMIAH DEFEATED THE DRAGON'S LURE

He Did Not Retaliate

He could have said, "Is that right, Tobiah? A little fox could push this wall down. Well, come on over here, you little weasel, and try to push it down yourself." No, there was none of that from Nehemiah. Retaliation never builds walls—but it does usually build *resentment*.

He Prayed

Hear, O our God, how we are despised! (Nehemiah 4:4).

Do not miss this: Nehemiah's lament before the throne disproves the modern-day saying, "Sticks and stones may break my bones, but words will never hurt me." Words, in fact, can cause deeper internal and longer-lasting wounds than many would ever admit. The truth is wounds of the heart last much longer than bruises on the arm or face. Nehemiah painfully lamented, "Are You listening, Lord? Are You hearing what they are saying?" Was Nehemiah surprised at the taunting words? No, but it still hurt him, and his prayer proves it:

> ***Return their reproach on their own heads and give them up for plunder in a land of captivity. Do not forgive their iniquity and let not their sin be blotted out before You, for they have demoralized the builders*** (Nehemiah 4:4b–5).

To interpret this prayer in its context, Nehemiah is praying from the vantage point of the Old Covenant—the dispensation of law. We don't pray this way in the New Covenant; we do not pray today that people will not find forgiveness. The Old Covenant was based upon the law, and the law was based upon retaliation. In that dispensation, to hate Jerusalem was to hate God; an enemy of Jerusalem was an enemy of God. The Old Testament saint would pray that God would enact vengeance upon his enemies on behalf of His character and glory and on behalf of the Holy City.

Nehemiah said nothing to his mockers; rather, he said everything to his Master. And he fully expected his Master to take care of his mockers because he knew that vengeance belongs to God *(Deuteronomy 32:35)*.

Convinced of this truth, Nehemiah did not retaliate, but he did pray.

He Continued Working

So we built the wall and the whole wall was joined together to half its height, for the people had a mind to work (Nehemiah 4:6).

Sticks and stones *may* break your bones, and words *will* hurt you. But that doesn't mean they have to *stop* you. Keep building the walls for the glory of God, the Champion who has ultimately defeated the old dragon.

Now when Sanballat, Tobiah, the Arabs, the Ammonites, and the Ashdodites heard that the repair of the walls of Jerusalem went on, and that the breaches began to be closed, they were very angry. [8]All of them conspired together to come and fight against Jerusalem and to cause a disturbance in it. [9]But we prayed to our God, and because of them we set up a guard against them day and night. [10]Thus in Judah it was said, "The strength of the burden bearers is failing, yet there is much rubbish; and we ourselves are unable to rebuild the wall." [11]Our enemies said, "They will not know or see until we come among them, kill them, and put a stop to the work." [12]When the Jews who lived near them came and told us ten times, "They will come up against us from every place where you may turn," [13]then I stationed men in the lowest parts of the space behind the wall, the exposed places, and I stationed the people in families with their swords, spears, and bows. [14]When I saw their fear, I rose and spoke to the nobles, the officials and the rest of the people: "Do not be afraid of them; remember the Lord who is great and awesome, and fight for your brothers, your sons, your daughters, your wives, and your houses." [15]When our enemies heard that it was known to us, and that God had frustrated their plan, then all of us returned to the wall, each one to his work. [16]From that day on, half of my servants carried on the work while half of them held the spears, the shields, the bows, and the breastplates; and the captains were behind the whole house of Judah. [17]Those who were rebuilding the wall and those who carried burdens took their load with one hand doing the work and the other holding a weapon. [18]As for the builders, each wore his sword girded at his side as he built, while the trumpeter stood near me. [19]I said to the nobles, the officials and the rest of the people, "The work is great and extensive, and we are separated on the wall far from one another. [20]At whatever place you hear the sound of the trumpet, rally to us there. Our God will fight for us." [21]So we carried on the work with half of them holding spears from dawn until the stars appeared. [22]At that time I also said to the people, "Let each man with his servant spend the night within Jerusalem so that they may be a guard for us by night and a laborer by day." [23]So neither I, my brothers, my servants, nor the men of the guard who followed me, none of us removed our clothes, each took his weapon even to the water.

—Nehemiah 4:7–23

CHAPTER EIGHT

HALFWAY!

Nehemiah 4:7–23

In World War II, as Germany prepared to invade Poland, the Poles readied themselves for battle. They were experienced warriors with a long history of repelling enemy attacks from barbarian neighbors. The Polish army was renowned for its skilled horsemanship—the Cavalry was well-trained and their horses were among Europe's finest steeds. When it was learned that German forces were advancing, twelve brigades of their finest were prepared. With swords flashing in the sunlight, the officers sounded the charge and their horses surged forward with powerful strides. Remember the time frame—World War II.

In his biography of Winston Churchill, Manchester wrote that the Cavalry galloped into oncoming, newly-designed German panzers. The outcome was predictable—total annihilation! Horsemen with swords were no match for armored tanks.

I am convinced that believers often expect to take on the forces of darkness with methods that rival galloping full speed into the path of an oncoming panzer division. The *devil, Lucifer, Satan, the deceiver, the father of lies, the great red dragon*, or any other biblical name you choose to use for the prince of hell is on a search and destroy mission. His weaponry is state-of-the-art, carefully selected, and adapted to each of his targets. His objective is to deceive, destroy, distract, and even divide any attempt by Christians to advance the kingdom of the Prince of heaven.

We have been warned:

Finally, be strong in the Lord and in the strength of His might. Put on the full armor of God, so that you may be able to stand firm against the schemes of the devil. For our struggle is not against flesh and blood, but against the rulers, against the powers, against the world forces of this darkness, against the spiritual forces of wickedness in the heavenly places. Therefore, take up the full armor of God, so that you will be able to resist in the evil day, and having done everything, to stand firm (Ephesians 6:10–13).

In other words, we are to be properly prepared for battle. We do not ride out on horseback to clash with German tanks. And we do not resist the great dragon with one hour of church and a brief blessing before lunch and dinner. We are to clothe ourselves in the armor of a warrior, which has been designed by God for the Christian champion.

FAITH—THE ESSENTIAL SHIELD

One of the pieces of armor designed by God that I so often depend upon in my own struggle with the enemy is the shield of faith. It is an essential weapon for any believer. I personally do not believe that these pieces of armor are merely defensive. All of them have an offensive element in resisting the temptation, the method, the scheme, and the lure of the great red dragon.

Paul describes one of the uses of the shield of faith:

[T]*aking up the shield of faith with which you will be able to extinguish all the flaming arrows of the evil one* (Ephesians 6:16).

The Object of Our Faith

When tested by battle conditions, our shield of faith has three important aspects:

1. **the living reality of God's Person –**

    David depended on this truth as he composed,

    But You, O LORD, are a shield about me (Psalm 3:3a).

2. **the reality of God's promises –**

Paul was confident as he wrote,
[T]*aking up the shield of faith with which you will be able to extinguish all the flaming arrows of the evil one* (Ephesians 6:16).

3. **the reality of God's providence –**

Paul could see through the haze of battle and take courage from his perspective,
And we know that God causes all things to work together for [our] *good . . . to become conformed to the image of His Son . . .* (Romans 8:28–29).

In other words, Paul encourages us to hold tightly the shield of faith— God is indeed behind every scene, engineering every detail and aspect of life toward the praise of His glory.

A few years ago, I was on the phone with a pastor. He was supposed to have returned my call the day before but had not called, so the next morning, I phoned him. Greetings were exchanged and then I asked, "Now, what about those dates we talked about? Are they going to work out?" I'll never forget his saying, "Boy, I don't know where my calendar is. Things are a little confusing right now—you see, my nine-year-old son was hit and killed by a car yesterday." I was speechless! As we talked, I was amazed by his confidence in the providence of God.

I remember being so personally convicted because the night before, I had been at the pharmacy. One of our daughters had a 104.6 degree temperature. Her mom had her in the bathtub, sponging her as I went out for medication. It was midnight, and I was thinking, *Lord, life is really lousy right now. Why can't this kind of thing happen after breakfast on my day off? Why can't You make this "trial" a little more convenient!*

My thoughts returned to the phone conversation. While I had been standing in that drugstore, complaining to the Lord about *convenience and timing*, that pastor had been kneeling over the lifeless form of his son. Yet, as he shared the events with me, it was so apparent that he and his wife were gripping the *shield of faith*.

In the thick of the battle, circumstances and challenges occur and, like a fiery missile, they are hurtled directly at your *faith*. These missiles often come in the form of whispered accusations: "Do you really believe that God is working everything out for *your good* and for *His glory*?" Perhaps it's more of a scream than a whisper: "Look at all you're going through! How could this be happening to you?" And do you find yourself agreeing with the accuser? "That's right. If the Father loved me, how could He be allowing *this* to happen?" Then, at that very time when you need your shield the most, you drop it, kick it aside, and leave yourself totally vulnerable to further attack.

If you are a Christian, the great dragon cannot steal your soul, but he can steal your song. Satan can never take God's love away from you, but he can make you *believe* that God does not love you.

The Operation of Our Faith

A closer look at this "Roman shield" to which Paul referred gives us insight into the operation of our faith as Christian soldiers.

- **It *protected* the soldier against the flaming arrows of the enemy.**

  There were two kinds of shields used by the Romans—a small circular shield that was used during hand-to-hand combat and a large oblong shield which completely covered the body of the soldier. In fact, this shield was often referred to as a door. It is this shield (*thureon* in the Greek language) that Paul is referring to in Ephesians. This was the large rectangular shield which a soldier could plant in the ground and hide behind. It was overlapped with leather and soaked with water so flaming arrows from enemy archers would hit the shield and simply fizzle out. It protected the soldier *and* his armor.

  Our confidence in God's person, promise, and providence protects us as believers from the fire of the great dragon.

- **It *unified* the army.**

  The Romans had invented this shield to be used collectively. The edges of the shields were beveled and notched so that they could be locked into place with the soldier next to them. You could actually have a row of men that made a wall of metal advancing against the enemy.

This is a tremendous illustration of what the Church should be doing—marching together with a unified purpose, passion, and heart. The shields of our hearts are joined together in the great cause of advancing the Gospel throughout enemy territory.

- **It *reflected* the sun.**

  In the center of each shield was a round piece of brass. Before going into battle, soldiers polished that brass so it shone with the brilliance of a mirror. As they walked into battle, they could reflect the light of the sun into the eyes of their enemies.

  We as believers also attempt to *reflect* the Lord Jesus Christ (the Light of the world) by our faith. Oh, how the dragon hates the name of Christ. He hates the reflection of Christ's Gospel: that Jesus Christ died and was buried but rose again on the third day—the brilliant light of the Gospel, which dispels the darkness. So when the dragon approaches, hide behind the shield while linking it to another believer's shield. Reflect on the attributes of God's *person*, the light of God's *promises*, and the security of God's *providence*.

NEHEMIAH—A MODEL OF FAITH

One of the most noble demonstrations of how to use the shield of faith is present in the life of Nehemiah. I invite you to pitch your tent with me just inside the city walls that are now halfway built. The forces of opposition have just added another army to their ranks:

> *Now when Sanballat, Tobiah, the Arabs, the Ammonites and the Ashdodites heard that the repair of the walls of Jerusalem went on, and that the breaches began to be closed, they were very angry. All of them conspired together to come and fight against Jerusalem and to cause a disturbance in it* (Nehemiah 4:7–8).

If you had a satellite picture of this scene around Jerusalem, you would notice that with the presence of the Ashdodites or Philistines to the west,

Jerusalem is now completely surrounded. Here's the reason why the enemies were so alarmed:

> *So we built the wall and the whole wall was joined together to half its height* (Nehemiah 4:6).

The walls were already *halfway up* when the enemies of God put together a concerted plan against Nehemiah and Jerusalem. What a strategic time for the enemy to turn up the heat. The Jewish people are now halfway finished, and that halfway point of any project is perhaps the most difficult to push past and keep forging ahead.

Whether you are running the mile or in a difficult semester or involved in a household renovation project where the mess looks bigger than the goal—*halfway* is a difficult hurdle in the course of life. The newness has worn off and the reality of the challenge has set in. Halfway is exactly where Nehemiah was in the project of rebuilding the wall when a popular notion begins to spread throughout the people:

> *Thus in Judah it was said, "The strength of the burden bearers is failing, yet there is much rubbish; and we ourselves are unable to rebuild the wall." Then I stationed men in the lowest parts of the space behind the wall, the exposed places, and I stationed the people in families with their swords, spears, and bows* (Nehemiah 4:10, 13).

In spite of all that had been accomplished up to this point, there was so much yet to do. Tired and weary, the people's original excitement to work had slowly given way to discouragement *in* the work. The source of this discontent? You guessed it—that old dragon had thrown out a new lure and the people had taken his deadly bait. Let's dissect this particular lure. It's one of Satan's most powerful tools. More believers have resigned the project and withdrawn to the sidelines because of discouragement—perhaps more than for any other reason. It would not be too surprising to discover that discouragement most often hits us at the halfway points in life.

DISSECTING DISCOURAGEMENT

It Usually Accompanies Physical Exhaustion

The strength of the burden bearers is failing (Nehemiah 4:10*a*).

Due to the immense labor exerted on the first half of the job, the people were physically worn out. This fatigue made them vulnerable prey for the enemy.

It Walks Hand-in-Hand with Distraction

Yet there is much rubbish (Nehemiah 4:10*b*).

A key word in this verse is *yet*. In other words, they were physically exhausted from the tremendous amount of work already accomplished, *yet* they glanced around and still saw rubbish, or literally "dry earth; debris."

Did you notice where the people had begun to focus their attention? Not on what had been completed, or on the progress they *had made*, but rather on all the work *yet to do*. There were piles of huge stones, overgrown vines, rubbish, and mounds of dirt. That was all they could see. Likewise, there are times—like raising children, accomplishing a demanding task at work, finishing a project, building a marriage, serving in a volunteer ministry position—when you can no longer see over the pile of rubbish. You ignore what has been accomplished and focus, instead, on what has not yet happened. It is the hurdle of being halfway.

It Produces Hopelessness

And we ourselves are unable to rebuild the wall (Nehemiah 4:10*c*).

If discouragement is allowed to run its course, it will result in giving up the struggle. "That's it, Nehemiah. We tried. We made it halfway, but we'll never make it to the top. It's a hopeless cause."

It Results in Fear

Our enemies said, "They will not know or see until we come among them, kill them and put a stop to the work." When the Jews who lived near them came and told us ten times, "They will come up against us from every place where you may turn" (Nehemiah 4:11–12).

Don't you just love these other Jews who live in the surrounding area? They **came and told us ten times** (Nehemiah 4:12a). "You'll never make it. You won't survive. The enemy is too numerous. No matter where you turn, they'll be waiting for you." (Thanks a lot, friends—your encouragement is heartwarming.)

Unfortunately, the people believed those discouraging, frightening words and acted accordingly—they left their work and fled for cover:

> *When I saw their fear, I rose and spoke to the nobles, the officials and the rest of the people: "Do not be afraid of them; remember the Lord who is great and awesome"* (Nehemiah 4:14a).

The people had compared their strength to the enemy's strength and had concluded: "We don't have a chance!" That was right, of course—*they*, in and of themselves, did not have strength equal to that of their enemies. Nehemiah, on the other hand, sized up the enemy's strength with the awesome power of God, not their own strength. In making this correct comparison, the enemies of Nehemiah had *no* chance against God, the mighty Warrior!

> *When our enemies heard that it was known to us, and that God had frustrated their plan, then all of us returned to the wall, each one to his work. From that day on, half of my servants carried on the work while half of them held the spears, the shields, the bows, and the breastplates; and the captains were behind the whole house of Judah. Those who were rebuilding the wall and those who carried burdens took their load with one hand doing the work and the other holding a weapon. As for the builders, each wore his sword girded at his side as he built, while the trumpeter stood near me. I said to the nobles, the officials, and the rest of the people, "The work is great and extensive, and we are separated on the wall far from one another. At whatever place you hear the sound of the trumpet, rally to us there. Our God will fight for us." So we carried on the work with half of them holding spears from dawn until the stars*

appeared. At that time I also said to the people, "Let each man with his servant spend the night within Jerusalem so that they may be a guard for us by night and a laborer by day." So neither I, my brothers, my servants, nor the men of the guard who followed me, none of us removed our clothes, each took his weapon even to the water (Nehemiah 4:15–23).

FOUR TIMELESS PRINCIPLES OF DEFENSE

1. **The people prayed to God.**

2. **The people prepared for battle.**

   Though their trust was in God, they still needed to prepare. As someone once said, "Petition without precaution is presumption." As Oliver Cromwell put it, "We will trust in God and keep our gunpowder dry." Ronald Reagan's famous quote during the Cold War was "Trust and verify."

3. **The people continued to build.**

   They went back to the wall and rejoined the task—the very thing the enemy wanted them to stop doing. They picked up their "shields of faith," and with their hearts trusting in God's faithfulness, they kept building that wall.

4. **The people pledged to defend one another.**

   At whatever place you hear the sound of the trumpet, rally to us there. Our God will fight for us (Nehemiah 4:20).

   Nehemiah's plan: "If you hear the trumpet, drop your tools and come running. We'll fight together, with the Lord's strength, wherever the enemy may attack." That's another way of saying, "Be prepared to link your shield of faith to the soldier next to you—no one fights alone."

Nehemiah's faith in the sovereign God empowered him to rally the people past their discouragement at the halfway point. For believers today, going *beyond* halfway will require a similar strategy.

PERSEVERING BEYOND HALFWAY

It Requires Spiritual Vision

This enables a person to envision the Lord high and lifted up. Without this perspective, we will focus on the circumstances and become discouraged. Spiritual vision causes us to remember that our God is an *awesome God*!

Martin Luther, the Reformer, had been struggling for weeks with discouragement. One day his wife entered his study dressed completely in black.

Martin asked, "Who died?"

She responded, "God has."

He stood to his feet and bellowed, "God has not died."

To which she responded, "Then stop acting as if He had."

It Demands Stubborn Faith

When your faith begins to wane before the goal is reached, remember the One who:

- so agonized in prayer that He sweat drops of blood;
- was despised, rejected, and crucified by the ones He loved;
- suffered so often that He was referred to as the "Man of Sorrows" who was acquainted with grief.

It Insists on Helping Others While Denying Self

The people began to diligently, selflessly serve one another:

- they were willing to rally together and fight for each other *(vs. 21a)*;
- they worked until the stars came out *(vs. 21b)*;
- they went without changing clothes or bathing *(vs. 23)*.

Nehemiah and the people were rescued from the lure of discouragement—the temptation to quit—and they continued building the walls of Jerusalem. Did you know that even to this day, everyone is involved in building one wall or another? Some people build a wall *between* themselves and others. Most tend to build walls *around* themselves. They build those walls high and thick, so no one can ever break through. They are satisfied with their lives behind the walls—no compassion for others, no ministry involvement in the lives of people. They are protected from the enemy. The truth is these people are not protected *from* the enemy; they have *become* their own enemy.

C. S. Lewis wrote,

> If you want to make sure of keeping your heart intact, you must give your heart to no one. Wrap it carefully round with hobbies and little luxuries; avoid all entanglements; lock it up safe in the coffin of your selfishness. But in that casket—safe, dark, motionless—it will change. It will not be broken; it will become unbreakable.

The enemy knows this all too well. He baits his hook with discouragement, and waits ever so patiently to see if a believer will take the lure and abandon the Savior's wall-work to focus on their own private world and enterprise. Have you taken the bait from the dragon's lure? How would you answer the following questions:

- Where is your focus today?
- Do you choose to look at all the things the Lord has already accomplished, or do you choose to look at the impossible things that have yet to be done?
- Are you relying on God's promises and provision that will enable you to prevail wherever He has you at work?
- Have you discarded your shield of faith, or are you faithfully reporting for "wall-duty"—shield, weapons, and all?
- Are you serving the needs of someone else, or are you serving only your personal needs?
- Finally, are you comparing the strength of your enemy to your own strength or to the omnipotence of the Father?

It's time to pick up your shield, take your position, and prepare to do battle . . . there's another half wall to be completed!

Now there was a great outcry of the people and of their wives against their Jewish brothers. ²For there were those who said, "We, our sons and our daughters are many; therefore let us get grain that we may eat and live." ³There were others who said, "We are mortgaging our fields, our vineyards and our houses that we might get grain because of the famine." ⁴Also there were those who said, "We have borrowed money for the king's tax on our fields and our vineyards. ⁵Now our flesh is like the flesh of our brothers, our children like their children. Yet behold, we are forcing our sons and our daughters to be slaves, and some of our daughters are forced into bondage already, and we are helpless because our fields and vineyards belong to others." ⁶Then I was very angry when I had heard their outcry and these words. ⁷I consulted with myself and contended with the nobles and the rulers and said to them, "You are exacting usury, each from his brother!" Therefore, I held a great assembly against them. ⁸I said to them, "We according to our ability have redeemed our Jewish brothers who were sold to the nations; now would you even sell your brothers that they may be sold to us?" Then they were silent and could not find a word to say. ⁹Again I said, "The thing which you are doing is not good; should you not walk in the fear of our God because of the reproach of the nations, our enemies? ¹⁰And likewise I, my brothers and my servants are lending them money and grain. Please, let us leave off this usury. ¹¹Please, give back to them this very day their fields, their vineyards, their olive groves and their houses, also the hundredth part of the money and of the grain, the new wine and the oil that you are exacting from them." ¹²Then they said, "We will give it back and will require nothing from them; we will do exactly as you say." So I called the priests and took an oath from them that they would do according to this promise. ¹³I also shook out the front of my garment and said, "Thus may God shake out every man from his house and from his possessions who does not fulfill this promise; even thus may he be shaken out and emptied." And all the assembly said, "Amen!" And they praised the Lord. Then the people did according to this promise. ¹⁴Moreover, from the day that I was appointed to be their governor in the land of Judah, from the twentieth year to the thirty-second year of King Artaxerxes, for twelve years, neither I nor my kinsmen have eaten the governor's food allowance. ¹⁵But the former governors who were before me laid burdens on the people and took from them bread and wine besides forty shekels of silver; even their servants domineered the people. But I did not do so because of the fear of God. ¹⁶I also applied myself to the work on this wall; we did not buy any land, and all my servants were gathered there for the work. ¹⁹Remember me, O my God, for good, according to all that I have done for this people.

—Nehemiah 5:1–16, 19

CHAPTER NINE

ME, MYSELF, AND I

Nehemiah 5

In our study of the book of Nehemiah, Satan has engineered several different attempts to cause the rebuilding work on the walls of Jerusalem to cease.

The enemies of God, spellbound by their evil master, have come against the children of Israel. The people of Jerusalem have had to contend with cruel mockery by the enemy. They've had to push past the halfway point when discouragement set in and nearly brought their work to a halt. Neither ridicule nor discouragement has been successful; in fact, the people of God have continued to labor . . . and the forces of darkness have continued their attack.

SATAN'S STRATEGY REVEALED

He Attempts to Discourage the Believer

Strategic moves in the form of persecution, intimidation, an insurmountable work load or, perhaps, a thorn in the flesh, which the Apostle Paul endured, may come our way. Paul told his friends that he was struggling with *a messenger of Satan* [sent] *to torment me* (2 Corinthians 12:7).

He Attempts to Deceive the Believer

This could come from false teachers—it could be the deception that causes you to think only about your life . . . to believe that God's work doesn't have a place for your gifts and that you aren't important to the cause of Christ. If Satan can't discourage believers and make them drop out of the race, if he can't deceive believers into accepting something that is not true and biblical, he will then try another strategy.

He Attempts to Divide Believers

Warren Wiersbe commented, "When the enemy fails in his attacks from the outside, he then begins to attack from within, and one of his favorite weapons is selfishness."

The enemy certainly used this approach in the first family, where one brother, envious and self-centered in his hatred, killed the other. Satan used it in the very first church, when an outcry came from Grecian believers because their older widows were not being cared for in the same way as the Hebrew widows. It created an incredible controversy within the flock at Jerusalem; it literally led to the redefining of church leadership. In another church—this one in Galatia—Paul had to remind them:

> But if you bite and devour one another, take care that you are not consumed by one another (Galatians 5:15).

Is it any wonder when conflict occurs among believers, Satan suddenly becomes neutral and simply supplies ammunition to both sides?

The worst enemy of the Church is, sadly, the Church itself; it is the thing that often keeps the Church from moving forward. New believers don't grow in Christ because "older" believers who have not matured become the primary stumbling block by their poor example. Likewise, the Church too often fails to reach out to the world because the world has reached inside the Church. Selfishness and Arrogance have become the Church's newest members. One of the Church's favorite hymns has shifted its focus from "God in Three Persons, blessed Trinity" to "God in Three Persons, Me, Myself, and I."

THE LURE OF SELFISHNESS

Selfishness is defined as having the attitude that people exist merely to meet my agenda, my wishes, and my needs; therefore, the value of anything (people, church, God, etc.), is determined only in light of what they do for me. This attitude is revealed not only in outward behavior but also in secret thought and, left unchecked, is ultimately destructive. Selfishness destroys friendships, marriages, ministries, and churches; it also destroys mission fields and other "sacred building projects" where God is clearly at work.

Recently, I received two separate phone calls from missionaries in different parts of the world. Both of these men said the most discouraging thing they faced on the field was "people problems"—strained relationships between team members.

Along this same line, a recent news report was given:

> Scores of people were hurt in a brawl during Sunday worship at a Kenyan church. The church had become divided into rival congregations by a dispute over its management decisions after church elders dismissed some church leaders on charges of financial irregularity. *The Kenya Times* said it took the intervention of police to stop part of the congregation from strangling a pastoral staff member appointed to take charge of running the church, which is located in the capital city of Nairobi. *The People* newspaper said members of the congregation turned their backs on the pulpit when the pastor attempted to lead in worship. For over four hours, many in the congregation booed, insulted, and heckled the pastor and scores of the faithful were left seriously injured when a free-for-all fist fight erupted.

This brought to mind a bumper sticker I saw on a car in front of me a few weeks ago. It included the name of a college with their motto underneath: "Fighting Christians." Obviously, it was not intended to convey the message that this college fought against Christians, but it struck me that it could be interpreted to refer to Christians who are fighting *one another!*

From the very first church in Jerusalem to the church in Corinth to the Church today, the greatest threat to the testimony and advancement of Christianity may very well be *Christians*. The Ephesian church also struggled with this problem, so Paul dedicated nearly an entire chapter to exhort them to simply get along and love one another. He pleaded with them to lay aside falsehood:

> *Speak truth each one of you with his neighbor, for we are members of one another. Be angry, and yet do not sin; do not let the*

sun go down on your anger; and do not give the devil an oppor-tunity (Ephesians 4:25–27).

These verses warn us that the devil is watching. He *longs* for this kind of selfish activity. To him it is a wonderful opportunity. He baits his hook with selfish advice: "Don't think about others, think only of yourself—your desires, your life, your money, your plans, your career, your retirement. Repeat after me" he says, "me, myself, and I . . . me, myself, and I!"

Paul's admonition to the Ephesian church included the command,

Let no unwholesome word proceed from your mouth, but only such a word as is good for edification according to the need of the moment, so that it will give grace to those who hear. Do not grieve the Holy Spirit of God, by whom you were sealed for the day of redemption. Let all bitterness and wrath and anger and clamor and slander be put away from you, along with all malice (Ephesians 4:29–31).

The implication was that Ephesian believers were involved in bitter disputes that included wrath, anger, and slander. Paul then instructed them as to the acceptable behavior of Christians:

Be kind to one another, tender-hearted, forgiving each other, just as God in Christ also has forgiven you (Ephesians 4:32).

These verses don't leave room for secret thoughts of selfishness, much less outward deeds of it.

Consider the fact that the very first sin came on the heels of the serpent telling Eve, in effect, "Think about *yourself*, Eve. This is something *you* want; if God really wanted to meet *your* needs, He'd let *you* have *your* way."

Thomas Merton was right when he wrote, "To consider people and events and situations only in the light of their effect upon you is to live on the doorstep of hell." There was a problem in Ephesus, Galatia, and Jerusalem. Today, there is a problem in Kenya, in England, in Syria, in America . . . in *my* town and in *yours*!

No believer, church, or country is exempt from it. We are all terminally infected with selfishness, and it lies at the core of every one of our sinful acts. That's why selfishness is such a productive and powerful weapon in Satan's arsenal. He will use it against us whenever he can. It must be dealt with and it must be battled against or it will destroy us all.

SATAN'S STRATEGY AGAINST NEHEMIAH

What happened in Jerusalem when self-centeredness momentarily brought the building project to a standstill?

> *Now there was a great outcry of the people and of their wives against their Jewish brothers. For there were those who said, "We, our sons and our daughters are many; therefore let us get grain that we may eat and live." There were others who said, "We are mortgaging our fields, our vineyards and our houses that we might get grain because of the famine." Also there were those who said, "We have borrowed money for the king's tax on our fields and our vineyards. Now our flesh is like the flesh of our brothers, our children like their children. Yet behold, we are forcing our sons and our daughters to be slaves, and some of our daughters are forced into bondage already, and we are helpless because our fields and vineyards belong to others"* (Nehemiah 5:1–5).

There are at least three problems represented in this eruption of controversy: hunger, debt, and high taxes. *Some things never change!*

NEHEMIAH'S COUNTER-STRATEGY AGAINST SATAN

There were four groups involved in the crisis:

1. People going hungry didn't own land to farm *(vs. 2)*.

2. People owning land had to mortgage their property in order to buy food *(vs. 3)*.

3. People owning land were so financially strapped that they were forced to borrow money in order to pay taxes *(vs. 4)*.

4. Wealthy Jewish leaders loaned their kinsmen money to take care of

the problem but for collateral took land and took children as slaves
(vs. 5).

The people had to choose between starvation or the slavery of their
children to wealthy Jews. The leaders and the wealthy were selfishly exploit-
ing the poorer people in order to make themselves even richer. It was, as
one author commented, an epidemic of selfishness and greed. How would
Nehemiah respond to this problem?

First, notice his *emotional* response:

> ***Then I was very angry when I had heard their outcry and
> these words*** (Nehemiah 5:6).

Next, his *physical* response is seen in three specific actions.

He Consulted with Himself

> ***I consulted with myself*** (Nehemiah 5:7*a*).

This literally means, "I took counsel within my own heart." Since
the leaders of Israel and the wealthy, powerful citizens were the problem,
Nehemiah couldn't really talk to any of them about this internal conflict. No
one carried this burden but Nehemiah.

He Confronted the High-Ranking Selfish Citizens

> [He] ***contended with the nobles and the rulers*** (Nehemiah
> 5:7*b*).

From a human standpoint, this was an incredible risk. At the very time
the enemies have surrounded Jerusalem and all of the workers are armed
with swords, Nehemiah is confronting the very men who could easily discourage the workers. If they became offended and angry at his confrontation
of their sin, these nobles and wealthy citizens might have packed their bags
and left the city. The loss of morale and unity would only add to Nehemiah's
problems. He could have chosen the easy road, taken a non-confrontational
approach and said, "Just go back to work—we'll figure out the food problem
later." Not Nehemiah; he was willing to confront them because he knew it
was the right thing to do.

He Challenged Their Selfishness

- ### *Selfish disobedience of* **Scripture**

  [He] *contended with the nobles and the rulers and said to them, "You are exacting usury* [interest], *each from his brother!" Therefore, I held a great assembly against them* (Nehemiah 5:7*b*).

The Old Testament made it clear that Jewish people could loan money and goods to other Jewish people, but they were not allowed to charge interest. In fact, every fifty years they were supposed to wipe any and every debt that they had against any other Jew off the books. It was called the Jubilee, and it kept the Jewish people from taking advantage of each other and becoming indebted to one another. These nobles and leading citizens have been charging interest. Later in the passage, we discover that it was 12 percent per year!

Nehemiah challenged them, "You are breaking the law, and you are doing it at the expense of your own brethren. You shouldn't be treating *family* like this."

- ### *Selfish violation of* **God's purpose for Israel**

  I said to them, "We according to our ability have redeemed our Jewish brothers who were sold to the nations; now would you even sell your brothers that they may be sold to us?" (Nehemiah 5:8*a*).

Nehemiah said, "God redeemed us from slavery and has brought us back to Jerusalem. How can you turn God's redemption upside down, betray, and enslave Jewish people again?" Their response was immediate (if you can call it a response):

Then they were silent and could not find a word to say (Nehemiah 5:8*b*).

This would have been a good stopping place for Nehemiah—right? These men know they have been greedy and selfish, and in front of the assembly, they are silenced. However, Nehemiah has one more point to deliver.

- *Selfish failure to* **represent God before unbelievers**

Is this not the heart of what is lost by those believers who act selfishly, vindictively, and without love toward one another? Nehemiah declared:

> *Again I said, "The thing which you are doing is not good; should you not walk in the fear of our God because of the reproach of the nations, our enemies? And likewise I, my brothers and my servants are lending them money and grain. Please, let us leave off this usury. Please, give back to them this very day their fields, their vineyards, their olive groves and their houses, also the hundredth part of the money and of the grain, the new wine and the oil that you are exacting from them"* (Nehemiah 5:9–11).

Nehemiah finished his speech and probably held his breath. How would they respond? Would their hearts be turned and softened? Would they put their loyalty to one another above the tremendous financial profit they were making off their own people? Or would they say, "I'm sorry" but continue looking for ways to take advantage of God's people? It's one thing to say, "I'm sorry, I won't be selfish any longer." It's quite another thing to say, "I'm sorry, I won't be selfish any longer—and I'm returning the money which I took from you." It is hard to imagine the kind of character that *returns* a fortune simply because it is the right thing to do.

I read with interest the story of Tim Forneris, the 22-year-old computer analyst who worked part-time as a groundskeeper for the St. Louis Cardinals. He was the one who retrieved Mark McGwire's 62nd home run ball. Then, to the shock of many and running counter to our American culture, he gave Mark McGwire the ball, saying that it belonged in the Hall of Fame instead of selling it to a collector who had offered one million dollars for the record-setting home run baseball. It was mind-boggling that someone would do that instead of cashing in on his good fortune. In fact, one well-known columnist called him, "honorable, but rather foolish."

Time magazine ran Tim's response, which shed light on his perspective:

> According to the columnist, my first sin was the impulsive decision to give the ball back to Mr. McGwire immediately. But my decision was, by no means, made on an impulse. I

had thought over what I would do if I got the home run ball and discussed it with my family and friends. What influenced my actions was my family and my background. I have always been taught to respect others and their accomplishments. In my opinion, Mr. McGwire deserved not only the home run record for his work, but also the ball. Life is about more than just money. It is about family and friends. I believe some possessions are priceless. To put an economic value on Mr. McGwire's hard work and dedication is absurd. And being able to return it to Mr. McGwire was an honor. I would not have traded that experience for one million dollars.

Imagine Nehemiah's response as the nobles of Jerusalem respond in the same way as Mr. Forneris:

> ***Then they said, "We will give it back and will require nothing from them; we will do exactly as you say"*** (Nehemiah 5:12*a*).

The next verse could easily have read, "Then they broke an ammonia capsule and passed it under his nose after observing that Nehemiah had fainted."

> ***So I called the priests and took an oath from them that they would do according to this promise*** (Nehemiah 5:12*b*).

NEHEMIAH'S UNSELFISH STRATEGY

So far, three things have happened that solidify their response:

1. They made a promise to Nehemiah.
2. They made a vow before the priests.
3. They demonstrated submission to God's authority.

However, Nehemiah was not quite satisfied:

> ***I also shook out the front of my garment and said, "Thus may God shake out every man from his house and from his possessions who does not fulfill this promise; even thus may he be shaken out and emptied." And all the assembly said,***

"Amen!" And they praised the Lord. Then the people did according to this promise (Nehemiah 5:13).

Unselfishness prompted a celebration. Generosity brought on a display of gratitude. They had a party right then and there. It works the same way even today: people who live unselfish lives encourage those around them to praise the Lord. Confetti is usually falling about now. Nehemiah was that kind of person. The rest of the chapter gives us his personal example of unselfish service before the people:

> *Moreover, from the day that I was appointed to be their governor in the land of Judah, from the twentieth year to the thirty-second year of King Artaxerxes, for twelve years, neither I nor my kinsmen have eaten the governor's food allowance. But the former governors who were before me laid burdens on the people and took from them bread and wine besides forty shekels of silver; even their servants domineered the people. But I did not do so because of the fear of God. I also applied myself to the work on this wall; we did not buy any land, and all my servants were gathered there for the work* (Nehemiah 5:14–16).

Do you get the picture here? Nehemiah was no ordinary ruler who lived off the labor of his subjects or took advantage of his position. He had every right to kick back in some ivory palace of pleasure and let the people do all the hard work. In fact, did you notice how verse 16 made it clear that Nehemiah was mixing mortar and hauling rock right along with the rest of them? Back then, that was *extremely* rare—as rare as it was for a young man in our day to give a million-dollar baseball back to the man who slammed it out of the park. Yet, in every generation, there are a few who do not live by the "Me, Myself, and I" rule.

Indeed, before the people, Nehemiah was *unselfish* in his service; before the Lord, he was *unwavering* in his worship:

> *Remember me, O my God, for good, according to all that I have done for this people* (Nehemiah 5:19).

Worship seeks the pleasure of God above all else. Selfish people want to be noticed by people. Nehemiah wanted to be noticed only by God. Did you observe that Nehemiah did *not* say, "O God, make those people around me appreciate my work" or "Lord, make my family respect my decision to live for You" or "God, make my friends and co-workers admire the decision I've made to pursue a holy life for Your glory." No, he said, "O my God, if you remember what I'm doing in obedience to You, that's enough for me."

Dr. Campbell, former president of Dallas Seminary, told the story of a young man who once studied violin under a world-renowned master. The time arrived for his debut. The performing arts center was filled with expectant observers and the media. Following each selection, despite the cheers of the crowd, the young man seemed dissatisfied. Even after the last number, when the shouts of "Bravo!" were the loudest, the talented violinist stood looking toward the balcony. Finally, an elderly man smiled and nodded in approval. Immediately, the young man relaxed and beamed with happiness.

Living for the approval of *our* Master has a way of making the applause of the world far less desirable . . . far less meaningful.

Now when it was reported to Sanballat, Tobiah, to Geshem the Arab and to the rest of our enemies that I had rebuilt the wall, and that no breach remained in it, although at that time I had not set up the doors in the gates, ²then Sanballat and Geshem sent a message to me, saying, "Come, let us meet together at Chephirim in the plain of Ono." But they were planning to harm me. ³So I sent messengers to them, saying, "I am doing a great work and I cannot come down. Why should the work stop while I leave it and come down to you?" ⁴They sent messages to me four times in this manner, and I answered them in the same way. ⁵Then Sanballat sent his servant to me in the same manner a fifth time with an open letter in his hand. ⁶In it was written, "It is reported among the nations, and Gashmu says, that you and the Jews are planning to rebel; therefore you are rebuilding the wall. And you are to be their king, according to these reports. ⁷You have also appointed prophets to proclaim in Jerusalem concerning you, 'A king is in Judah!' And now it will be reported to the king according to these reports. So come now, let us take counsel together." ⁸Then I sent a message to him saying, "Such things as you are saying have not been done, but you are inventing them in your own mind." ⁹For all of them were trying to frighten us, thinking, "They will become discouraged with the work and it will not be done." But now, O God, strengthen my hands. ¹⁰When I entered the house of Shemaiah the son of Delaiah, son of Mehetabel, who was confined at home, he said, "Let us meet together in the house of God, within the temple, and let us close the doors of the temple, for they are coming to kill you, and they are coming to kill you at night." ¹¹But I said, "Should a man like me flee? And could one such as I go into the temple to save his life? I will not go in." ¹²Then I perceived that surely God had not sent him, but he uttered his prophecy against me because Tobiah and Sanballat had hired him. ¹³He was hired for this reason, that I might become frightened and act accordingly and sin, so that they might have an evil report in order that they could reproach me. ¹⁴Remember, O my God, Tobiah and Sanballat according to these works of theirs, and also Noadiah the prophetess and the rest of the prophets who were trying to frighten me. ¹⁵So the wall was completed on the twenty-fifth of the month Elul, in fifty-two days. ¹⁶When all our enemies heard of it, and all the nations surrounding us saw it, they lost their confidence; for they recognized that this work had been accomplished with the help of our God.

—Nehemiah 6:1–16

CHAPTER TEN

PSST . . . HAVE YOU HEARD?

Nehemiah 6

I n our study of the book of Nehemiah, we have observed how Satan has attempted to stop Nehemiah from rebuilding the city of God. Some attacks have come from the outside in the form of ridicule, fear, and discouragement, while other problems have sprung up from the inside resulting in division, anger, and betrayal. In **Nehemiah 6**, the dragon apparently pulls out all the stops and launches one attack after another. They are painful, heart-wrenching, and discouraging to Nehemiah. The attacks will come from both the outside and the inside. It will be the loneliest and most fearful moments that Nehemiah will encounter as he handles one threat after another.

For the believer today, there is one particular piece of armor that seems to get less attention than the others. However, it will be this piece—*the helmet of salvation*—that is available to every believer that will, above all others, protect Nehemiah against the assault of the enemy, for this vital piece protects the *mind* of the Christian.

Cyril Barber, in his book on Nehemiah, makes a point that there are three areas in the believer's life that Satan attacks regularly, and each of the three areas relates directly to our relationship to the Three Persons of the Godhead. He wrote that our relationship with God the Father gives us:

1. **a sense of belonging** – We are sons and daughters of His family, and

we are secure in our Father/child relationship.

2. **a sense of worth** – God loves us so much that He sent His Son to die for our sins. With our redemption accomplished, we actually become joint heirs with Jesus Christ. Our union with Christ, the Son of God, shows us our incredible worth and value to God.

3. **a sense of competence** – The Holy Spirit's indwelling empowers us to live for Jesus Christ. We are made equal to every task, and through His strength we can fulfill whatever God designs for us to do.

Our *belonging*, our *worth*, and our *competency* are directly related to our union with God. Satan loves nothing more than to attack us on these three fronts. He artfully aims at our sense of security (belonging), our sense of value to God and the church (worth), and our sense of strength and skill for the task (competency). If he's successful, the believer is paralyzed with doubt and fear. The piece of armor that combats those attacks and protects us on all of these battlegrounds is the helmet of salvation. Reflecting, remembering, and acknowledging the biblical truth of our redemption and our relationship with each Person of the Godhead protects our minds against these lies of the great dragon.

Nehemiah will face his most difficult battles yet, because they are primarily battles that will require biblical thinking. It will require his *emotions* and *will* to be saturated by truths that he already knows—those about who God is, and who he is. They will be the toughest battles recorded in his memoirs. One commentator even referred to **Nehemiah 6** as "a battle of nerves." Let's find out why.

THE DRAGON'S FULL-SCALE ATTACK

Because none of the previous lures had stopped the rebuilding of the wall, the enemy now fires multiple, varied, and intense missiles in an effort to stop this work, once and for all.

Incoming Missile 1: Create Confusion

Now when it was reported to Sanballat, Tobiah, to Geshem the Arab, and to the rest of our enemies that I had rebuilt the wall, and that no breach remained in it, although at that time I had not set up the doors in the gates, then Sanballat and Geshem sent a message to me, saying, "Come, let us meet together at Chephirim in the plain of Ono." But they were planning to harm me. So I sent messengers to them, saying, "I am doing a great work and I cannot come down. Why should the work stop while I leave it and come down to you?" They sent messages to me four times in this manner, and I answered them in the same way (Nehemiah 6:1–4).

Did you notice the timing of this request? Verse one reveals that the walls are finished, but *the gates have not been hung*. It is the last possible moment for the enemy to stop the work from being completed. It is also the best time for Nehemiah to feel somewhat confident that the project is actually going to be completed. Now, rather surprisingly, a request arrives from his enemies in the form of a polite invitation to begin dialoguing:

"Come, let us meet at . . . Ono" (Nehemiah 6:2).

Ono was an oasis—a retreat location for the wealthy. It had fertile land with trees and water. "Come on, Nehemiah, we've dogged your heels; it's been a tough battle and now that it's over and you've won, let's get together and talk it over; why not relax for just a day or two?" *Four times* they asked if he wanted an all-expense-paid vacation at the Ono Resort and Spa. And all four times Nehemiah said the same thing, "No, I won't go to Ono!"

This action made him run the risk of being called cold and heartless. After all, while *he* discerned that Sanballot, Tobiah, and the others were trying to trick him, no one else recognized the plot. These "kind" invitations were an attempt to create confusion. Outwardly, it looked like they wanted to make amends, talk it over, and reach an agreement. But underneath was a different motive, as Nehemiah revealed in his diary:

But they were planning to harm me (Nehemiah 6:2*b*).

One author imagines what the newspapers would have said, had they printed the account in Nehemiah's day:

> From Samaritan sources it is learned that Governor Nehemiah of Judah has again turned down the invitation of Sanballat, head of the district of Samaria, to come to the village of Ono for a conference of the big four: Gashmu, leader of the Edomites; Tobiah, leader of the Ammonites; Sanballat; Nehemiah. Sanballat issued an announcement today in which

he sharply criticized Nehemiah for his repeated refusal to appear at such a meeting—the purpose of which, according to Sanballat, is "simply to adjust the relations among these rulers and bring about peace in the area."

The next week, another article would appear:

> The Samaritan leader claims this is the fourth time that Nehemiah has asked for a postponement of the conference on the grounds that he is too busy. This, despite the fact that Ono, the place designated as the site of the meeting, is no more than a four and a half hour ride from Jerusalem. "The responsibility for anything that may happen and for the blood that may be shed rests solely upon Nehemiah," the announcement concludes.

The truth was this diplomatic invitation was actually a deadly letter of deceit. For reasons known only to God, Nehemiah was able to discern that this was a trap, and his answer to them four times was, "No!" While the invitation was intended to cause confusion about the true motive of the enemy, Nehemiah was willing to run the risk of being misunderstood.

Have you learned to say the word *no*? I highly recommend it. This word should be said more often to television commercials, two-year-olds and, most importantly . . . *temptation.*

Incoming Missile 2: Create Scandal

Then Sanballat sent his servant to me in the same manner a fifth time with an open letter in his hand. In it was written, "It is reported among the nations, and Gashmu says, that you and the Jews are planning to rebel; therefore you are rebuilding the wall. And you are to be their king, according to these reports. You have also appointed prophets to proclaim in Jerusalem concerning you, 'A king is in Judah!' And now it will be reported to the king according to these reports. So come now, let us take counsel together" (Nehemiah 6:5–7).

Their strategy was, "Since we can't *trick* Nehemiah, let's *discredit* him. Let's tell everyone that Nehemiah wants to rebuild Jerusalem just so he can sit on the throne and be the king." This letter hit like a bombshell. It started a rumor that had the potential of totally destroying Nehemiah's credibility—which is precisely what they wanted to do. Can you imagine how this news riffled through the camp? "Nehemiah wants to be the king of Jerusalem—that's been his purpose all along!"

Frankly, the more interesting the gossip, the more likely it is to be untrue—and yet the faster it will be spread. There is something in each of us which prompts us to believe things that are whispered in our ear. Any sentence that begins with the words, *"Psst, have you heard?"* is sure to get the full attention of the listener. And once it is out, it spreads like wildfire. Many times the damage is irrevocably done. Trying to squash a rumor is like trying to unring a bell. Is it any wonder that of the seven things that God hates mentioned in the book of Proverbs, three of them have to do with *the tongue*?

> *Then I sent a message to him saying, "Such things as you are saying have not been done, but you are inventing them in your own mind"* (Nehemiah 6:8).

If you have ever been gossiped about or had rumors spread about you, you can learn a lot from Nehemiah's response. He did *not* say, "Here are ten reasons why you are wrong, and I can explain why some misguided prophets are announcing that I'm the next king of Jerusalem, but I haven't hired them." Instead, we find a total absence of self-defense. There is no long letter in return and no self-vindication. There was only the simple reply, "It's not true. You've made it up." Even after the missile exploded around him, Nehemiah saw the true intention of his enemy:

> *For all of them were trying to frighten us, thinking, "They will become discouraged with the work and it will not be done"* (Nehemiah 6:9a).

Unfortunately, the gossip spread and many in Jerusalem became suspicious of Nehemiah. In fact, later in this chapter we discover that the leaders of the tribe of Judah believed the rumor and added their own words of distrust for Nehemiah.

Leaders are vulnerable to this sort of attack—a flippant question about their integrity; an off-handed remark by someone who challenges the leader's motive; an angry response toward a leader's decision they found not to their liking; the jealousy of another who would enjoy seeing the work hindered. The reputation of the leader is sullied. The bad news is that there is no insurance policy available for injuries caused by word of mouth. Of all the challenges Nehemiah faced, this personal attack on his character and his motive for ministry was the attack that truly wounded this good soldier. Listen as an injured Nehemiah cried out in the only way a true leader should ever respond:

But now, O God, strengthen my hands (Nehemiah 6:9*b*).

Nehemiah, with his tough exterior and his nothing-is-too-big-to-tackle attitude has finally been injured by the enemies' blows. He knows that he cannot move forward without renewed strength from Jehovah. This fiery missile which targeted Nehemiah's character had found its mark and brought intense pain. Nevertheless, Nehemiah will *not* give up but, rather, he cries out to God for renewed strength.

As evidenced by Nehemiah, gossip is a dangerous weapon in the enemies' hands. It can bring down a ministry and a minister when other weapons have been useless against him.

Here's a brief bio of the culprit:

> I have no respect for justice. I maim without killing. I break hearts and ruin lives. I am cunning and malicious and gather strength the older I am alive. The more I am quoted, the more I am believed. My victims are helpless. They cannot protect themselves against me because I have no name and no face. To track me down is impossible. The harder you try, the more elusive I become. I topple governments and wreck friendships. I ruin careers and cause sleepless nights and heartaches. I make innocent people cry in their pillows. I make headlines and headaches. I am nobody's friend. Even my name hisses. I am *Gossip*.

How do we protect our church, our families, and our work ethic from the erosion brought about by the tongue? How can we make sure that we are not part of the enemy's arsenal used against someone else?

Alan Redpath once pastored the large Moody Church in Chicago and wrote how he encouraged the members of his church during a particularly stressful time in their church history. It was to practice a simple formula before speaking. Since he wanted them to think before speaking, he gave them an acrostic: THINK.

T – Is it *true?*

H – Is it *helpful?*

I – Is it *inspirational?*

N – Is it *necessary?*

K – Is it *kind?*

If it did not pass the THINK test, it was not spoken to another person. That is good advice for the Church, as well as for all areas of life. If your speech is running down your co-workers or your boss, you are wrong. As a believer, you have no business working with that attitude. If you are speaking out loud against spiritual leaders or members of your own church, stop and *think*. The THINK test will revolutionize your work environment, and it just may revolutionize your home and your church environment, as well.

The enemies of Nehemiah and of the work of God said, "Let's confuse him"; then, "Let's discredit him." But God strengthened the hands and heart of Nehemiah to keep on building.

Incoming Missile 3: Create Compromise

When I entered the house of Shemaiah the son of Delaiah, son of Mehetabel, who was confined at home, he said, "Let us meet together in the house of God, within the temple, and let us close the doors of the temple, for they are coming to kill you, and they are coming to kill you at night" (Nehemiah 6:10).

This warning sounded good on the surface. Besides, it came from a priest. In fact, he was a prophet *and* a priest. The English translation obscures the fact that this warning came in the form of a prophecy, as if it came from God. Imagine somebody telling you, "Listen, I overheard that some of your enemies are coming over tonight and they're going to kill you. You'd better hide." Imagine trying to sleep after hearing that—you would hear every creaking floor joist, every chirping cricket, every rustling leaf.

So this priest says to Nehemiah, "Listen, I have received word from God that your enemies are coming to kill you. You need to come over to the temple, and we'll hide out together in the holy place." As authentic as it sounded, Nehemiah saw through the phony prophecy:

But I said, "Should a man like me flee? And could one such as I go into the temple to save his life? I will not go

in." Then I perceived that surely God had not sent him, but he uttered his prophecy against me because Tobiah and Sanballat had hired him. He was hired for this reason, that I might become frightened and act accordingly and sin, so that they might have an evil report in order that they could reproach me (Nehemiah 6:11–13).

Was it a sin for Nehemiah to be afraid? No. Was it a sin for Nehemiah to hide during the night? No. But if you look closely, you will notice that Shemaiah proposed that they hide out in the *holy place*—where only priests could enter. For Nehemiah to go into the holy place, even though it might save his life, would have violated the law of God. *Nehemiah would rather lose his life than to sin.*

How much sin will you allow in your life before you become even a little bit bothered? Here is a man who would rather risk his life than risk losing the pleasure of God in his life. Nehemiah's response provides great insight into determining good counsel from bad. Here are three things to ask yourself:

1. Does the counsel violate your conscience?
2. Does the counsel contradict Scripture?
3. Does the counsel hinder your commitment?

If *yes* is the answer to any of these questions, the counsel should *not* be heeded.

During the excruciatingly painful events of these attacks, you would think that Nehemiah must have felt the urge to retaliate against those men who were discrediting his character. But instead, Nehemiah boldly prayed,

> *Remember, O my God, Tobiah and Sanballat according to these works of theirs, and also Noadiah the prophetess and the rest of the prophets who were trying to frighten me* (Nehemiah 6:14).

Rather than seeking vengeance for himself, he prayed and asked *God* to remember their deeds and act against them accordingly.

Incoming Missile 4: Create Division

The frustrated enemies of Nehemiah said, "We can't trick him, discredit him, or tempt him; so let's *abandon* him."

Also in those days many letters went from the nobles of Judah to Tobiah, and Tobiah's letters came to them. For many in Judah were bound by oath to him because he was the son-in-law of Shecaniah the son of Arah, and his son Jehohanan had married the daughter of Meshullam the son of Berechiah. Moreover, they were speaking about his good deeds in my presence and reported my words to him. Then Tobiah sent letters to frighten me (Nehemiah 6:17–19).

I personally couldn't take one week of this, but Nehemiah endured it for *months*. Tobiah was the enemy of God's work, but here you have prophets, a prophetess, and leaders in Judah who were constantly telling Nehemiah what a great man Tobiah was. "C'mon, Nehemiah, you need to get over your problem with Tobiah. He's really doing us all a favor. We need him around here." Yet all the while, according to the last part of **Nehemiah 6:19**, Tobiah is sending letters to Nehemiah to try to scare him away.

You could circle a word that appears several times throughout this chapter: *frighten*. The enemies of God constantly tried to frighten Nehemiah into quitting. But he just *would not quit* building the wall:

So the wall was completed on the twenty-fifth of the month Elul, in fifty-two days. When all our enemies heard of it, and all the nations surrounding us saw it, they lost their confidence; for they recognized that this work had been accomplished with the help of our God (Nehemiah 6:15–16).

Can you imagine any sweeter words than *so the wall was completed*?! "The wall is finished, put away your tools, take down the scaffolding, swing the massive gates shut, and bolt them tightly. By the help of our faithful God, we have *finished* the work."

Though the dragon waged an all-out, gloves-off, last-ditch effort to stop the work, God faithfully protected His work and lovingly strengthened His workers, and He will do the same for us today. When believers resist the lure of the devil and keep on building, two things will eventually happen.

NEHEMIAH'S FULL-SCALE VICTORY

Think about it—for ninety years the people of Judah had not been able to do it. But this time, the people had their hearts in the work, and they had a leader who would not quit. I can only imagine the celebration as the nations around them realized that all their plotting, planning, intimidating, and rumor-mongering had utterly failed. Did you notice the result of that finished wall?

> **When all our enemies heard of it, and all the nations sur-**
> **rounding us saw it, they lost their confidence;** [Why?] **for**
> **they recognized that this work had been accomplished . . .**
> (Nehemiah 6:16).

Was it because of Nehemiah's leadership? Because the people were skilled at building? Maybe the conditions were favorable and the king of Persia had provided lumber for the gates? No.

> **[T]his work had been accomplished with the help of our**
> **God** (Nehemiah 6:16).

These unbelievers knew that *Someone* supernatural was involved for the walls to have been rebuilt in just *fifty-two days.*

What a way to live! Stay at the hard labor of building families, marriages, homes, and ministries so that those around us can only explain the results in terms of *God's* involvement. That is vindication enough.

What is the result of overcoming these missiles from the enemy? Simply put, God is glorified and His cause is galvanized. Is it, therefore, any wonder that Satan battles whatever God builds? Is it any surprise then that there are no opportunities for the kingdom of heaven without opposition from the kingdom of hell? Expect it! Be alert to it! Paul reminds us as we attempt to build something for the kingdom of light:

> For our struggle is not against flesh and blood, but against the
> rulers, against the powers, against the world forces of this dark-
> ness, against the spiritual forces of wickedness in the heavenly
> places (Ephesians 6:12).

So keep building the walls of character, marriage, personal holiness, godly friendships, and authentic witness before unbelievers. And remember while you're at it, missiles are incoming.

Dudley Tyng was the son of a well-known and successful preacher. After his father's retirement, young Tyng followed him, filling the pulpit at the Church of the Epiphany in Philadelphia. He was an outspoken, powerful, uncompromising preacher with great influence on spiritual leaders around him. In addition to weekly worship services, Pastor Tyng would also hold meetings for men at the local YMCA during weekday lunch hours.

In order to reach more men for Christ, he organized a rally on March 30, 1858. Five thousand men came! During the message the 29-year-old shouted: "I would rather this right arm were amputated at the trunk than that I should come short of my duty to you in delivering God's message." He was preaching from Exodus 10:11 on the text "Ye that are men, go and serve the Lord." One thousand men accepted Christ as their Savior that day.

Two weeks later he was visiting the countryside, watching a corn thrasher in a barn. He moved his hand too close to the machine, and his arm was ripped from its socket. Four days later his arm was amputated. As he was dying, he told his old father, "Stand up for Jesus, father, and tell my brethren of the ministry to stand up for Jesus."

Pastor George Duffield was stirred by the funeral and preached the next Sunday from *Ephesians 6* about standing firm. In this message he read a poem that he had written, having been inspired at the funeral. This has become one of America's favorite hymns, now sung by millions.

> *Stand up, stand up for Jesus, ye soldiers of the cross!*
> *Lift high His royal banner—it must not suffer loss.*
> *From victory unto victory His army shall He lead;*
> *ll every foe is vanquished and Christ is Lord indeed.*
>
> *Stand up, stand up for Jesus, stand in His strength alone;*
> *The arm of flesh will fail you—ye dare not trust your own.*
> *Put on the gospel armor, each piece put on with prayer;*
> *Where duty calls or danger, be never wanting there.*
>
> *Stand up, stand up for Jesus, the strife will not be long;*
> *This day the noise of battle—the next, the victor's song.*
> *To him that overcometh a crown of life shall be;*
> *He with the King of glory shall reign eternally.*

What a way to battle alongside your triumphant Dragon Slayer.

Now when the wall was rebuilt and I had set up the doors, and the gatekeepers and the singers and the Levites were appointed, ²then I put Hanani my brother, and Hananiah the commander of the fortress, in charge of Jerusalem, for he was a faithful man and feared God more than many. ³Then I said to them, "Do not let the gates of Jerusalem be opened until the sun is hot, and while they are standing guard, let them shut and bolt the doors. Also appoint guards from the inhabitants of Jerusalem, each at his post, and each in front of his own house." ⁴Now the city was large and spacious, but the people in it were few and the houses were not built. ⁵Then my God put it into my heart to assemble the nobles, the officials and the people to be enrolled by genealogies. Then I found the book of the genealogy of those who came up first in which I found the following record:

—Nehemiah 7:1–5

CHAPTER ELEVEN

ROLL THE CREDITS

Nehemiah 7:1–5

E ugene Petersen wrote these challenging words in his book entitled *Run with the Horses*:

> There is little to admire and less to imitate in the people who are prominent in our culture. We have celebrities but not saints. Neither the adventure of goodness nor the pursuit of righteousness gets headlines. If, on the other hand, we look around for what it means to be a person of integrity, we don't find much. They aren't easy to pick out. No journalist interviews them. No talk show features them. They're not admired. They're not looked up to. They do not set trends. There is no cash value in them. No Oscars are given for integrity. At year's end, no one compiles a list of "The Ten Best-Lived Lives."

The world does not notice lives that *ought* to be noticed. For the most part, neither does the Church. Frankly, part of our fallen nature, as people, is to take each other for granted and to ignore the accomplishments and service that benefit all of us. They are all around us, but we rarely notice.

Take mothers, for example—I recently read the following:

> A man came home from work to find total mayhem in his house. His three children were outside, still in their pajamas, playing in the dirt with empty cookies boxes and candy wrappers strewn all around the front yard. The door to his wife's SUV was open,

as was the front door to the house. Proceeding into the entry, he found an even bigger mess. A lamp had been knocked over and the throw rug was wadded up against one wall. In the family room, the TV was loudly blaring, and the living room was littered with toys and items of clothing. In the kitchen, dishes filled the sink, breakfast food was spilled on the counter, dog food was scattered on the floor, a broken glass lay under the table, and a small pile of sand was spread by the back door.

He quickly ran upstairs, stepping over toys and more piles of clothes, looking for his wife, worried that she was ill or that something serious had happened. He discovered her in the bedroom, still curled up in bed in her pajamas, reading a novel. There was a half-eaten bagel and two coffee cups on the bedside stand. She looked up and asked how his day went. He looked at her, bewildered, and asked, "What happened here today?"

She smiled and answered, "You know, every day when you come home from work, you ask me what in the world did I do all day? Well, today I didn't do it."

It's unfortunate and yet true that even those closest to you will never fully comprehend the scope of your labor and toil, nor will they take the time to discover it. Think about it—when was the last time you watched a movie and then stayed around to watch the credits as they rolled by? What about that beautiful musical score that touched you so much—did you look to see who composed it? No. The film's over; time to move on to the next event in life.

I find it absolutely fascinating that at the end of chapter six, when the show is over, so to speak, and the walls are built, Nehemiah takes time to roll the credits. The list is long and most of the names are unpronounceable. But there are some gems tucked inside these credits that God considers profitable for every student of the Bible. So, before you are tempted to pick up your popcorn bucket and candy wrappers, let's take time to notice some of the men and women who were part of this incredible story of God's faithfulness.

We will concentrate on **Nehemiah 7** but also keep our finger at **Nehemiah 11**, which has another divinely inspired list of names and numbers—all representing many behind-the-scenes people who finished the Jerusalem project.

SINGERS

Now when the wall was rebuilt and I had set up the doors, and the gatekeepers and the singers and the Levites were appointed, then I put Hanani my brother, and Hananiah the commander of the fortress, in charge of Jerusalem (Nehemiah 7:1–2).

[T]he sons of Asaph, who were the singers for the service of the house of God. For there was a commandment from the king concerning them and a firm regulation for the song leaders day by day (Nehemiah 11:22–23).

Remember, for years the people of Israel had been in captivity, and then for a century beyond that, had been in a foreign land. During this time, all singing had *ceased*. In fact, *Psalm 137* tells us that they sat down and *wept* by the rivers of Babylon. They hung up their harps on the branches of the willow trees and stopped singing. Yet in the Book of Nehemiah, they began once again tuning up their instruments. It is noteworthy that Nehemiah makes eight references to giving thanks to God through song. Music is not *incidental* to worship—it is *essential* to worship.

On the occasion of Dallas Theological Seminary's fiftieth anniversary, the seminary published a special hymnal titled *Hymns of Jubilee*. Dr. Edwin Deibler wrote the following prologue in the hymnal:

> From earliest times, the people of God have employed music to give expression of their adoration of the triune God. Succeeding generations of Christians, to our present day, have adopted poetry set to music to express their adoration, praise, aspirations, and prayer. Often, perhaps nearly always, such expressions have exceeded in intensity the actual lifestyles of the congregations who employed them. If Christian experience were, even for a period of one week, brought to the level of Christian hymns, a great revival would sweep over the world.

I find it fascinating that *before* revival occurs in **Nehemiah 8**, choir memberships are renewed in chapter seven.

GATEKEEPERS

While the singers provided the praise for the city of Jerusalem, the gate-keepers provided protection:

> **Also the gatekeepers, Akkub, Talmon and their brethren who kept watch at the gates, were 172** (Nehemiah 11:19).

I can imagine the following conversation:

"Hey, Akkub and Talmon, what great role do you play in the kingdom?"

"We open and shut the gates, and then, we watch to make sure nobody gets in who shouldn't."

Imagine 172 keepers at the gate.

The Great Wall of China was breached by invaders at various times. Most famously, Genghis Khan reportedly said, "The strength of the wall depends on the courage of those who defend it" and then breached it by bribing a sentry. *Gates are only as good as the character of the guards.*

Were you aware that every believer in Christ is also a gatekeeper?

John Bunyan, the author of *Pilgrim's Progress*, also wrote a book entitled *The Holy War*. In that book he talked about Mansoul, a city with five gates. The gates were:

1. The Ear Gate
2. The Eye Gate
3. The Nose Gate
4. The Feel Gate
5. The Mouth Gate

The enemy of Mansoul daily attacked at one of the gates. He spoke through the Ear Gate or painted vivid and alluring pictures for the Eye Gate. The interesting thing is that Mansoul, the city in Bunyan's allegory, could *never* be toppled by outside attacks. The only way it could be conquered was if someone on the inside opened one of the gates to the enemy.

Solomon warned,

> *Watch over your heart with all diligence, for from it flow the springs of life* (Proverbs 4:23).

In other words, guard carefully what you allow through the gates of your life that will ultimately impact your heart and soul. Be a diligent, vigilant gatekeeper.

ADMINISTRATORS

Nehemiah knew that he needed help leading the city of Jerusalem, so he chose two men:

> *I put Hanani my brother, and Hananiah the commander of the fortress, in charge of Jerusalem* (Nehemiah 7:2).

At this point, the walls are up, the doors are hung, and now Nehemiah needs someone to help him lead the city government and its people. Who would you look for? Probably someone with experience—that makes sense. Someone who has the stature and bearing that people automatically follow—also, a logical choice. If you're looking for someone to command, they need to know how to be a commander, right? Wrong on all counts. We are given only two qualifications that Nehemiah was looking for:

> *For he was a faithful man and feared God more than many* (Nehemiah 7:2*b*).

The Hebrew word translated *feared* comes from *yare*, which means "to reverence or to honor."

What a great lesson for the Church and any other missionary enterprise. We tend to follow the world's example in looking for people to fill the slots, appointments, and key ministry positions. We look for people who are experienced, who look good on the outside, who can communicate and articulate the party line, and who have a bearing about them that draws attention to their winsome personalities and natural abilities.

Notice that the two qualities Nehemiah mentioned would not usually appear on someone's resumé. These were qualities of dependability and reverence for God.

CITIZENS

The next part of the chapter finds Nehemiah registering the citizens. They were identified and counted according to family, clan, or tribe:

> *The sons of Parosh, 2,172; the sons of Shephatiah, 372; the*
> *sons of Arah, 652; the sons of Pahath-moab of the sons of*
> *Jeshua and Joab, 2,818; the sons of Elam, 1,254* (Nehemiah
> 7:8–12).

Why count them so carefully? They were counted *by* God because they
counted *to* God.

PRIESTS

The priests had to prove their lineage to Aaron or they would not be
allowed to serve in the temple:

> *These were they who came up from Tel-melah, Tel-harsha,*
> *Cherub, Addon and Immer; but they could not show their*
> *fathers' houses or their descendants, whether they were of Israel*
> *. . . These searched among their ancestral registration, but it*
> *could not be located; therefore they were considered unclean*
> *and excluded from the priesthood* (Nehemiah 7:61, 64).

The same requirement was enforced upon the people: if they could
not trace their family lineage back to pre-dispersion ancestors, they were
excluded from living inside the city walls. God enforced a high standard for
owning land within the city of Jerusalem and for serving in the temple. You
had to have Jewish blood flowing through your veins, and you had to have
written proof of your genealogy.

This leads to some important questions. What right do you have to live
within the gates of the *new* Jerusalem? The Book of Revelation tells us that
only those redeemed by Jesus Christ will be able to dwell in the Holy City of
heaven. Will you be able to trace your lineage back to the family of God? Are
you related to God through faith in His Son, Jesus Christ? Jesus announced,

> *"Many will say to me on that day, 'Lord, Lord, did we not*
> *prophesy in Your name, and in Your name cast out demons, and*
> *in Your name perform may miracles?' And then I will declare to*
> *them, 'I never knew you'"* (Matthew 7:22–23a).

The pressing questions in *Nehemiah 7* and *11*, were: Did the inhabitants have a bloodline to Israel? Could they prove their relationship to the
people of *the* one true God? The pressing question in the last day of human

history, as we know it, will be, "Are you related to that Jewish Carpenter—the true Messiah? Can you prove your relationship to the family of God?"

God is also keeping a list of names. It is called the Lamb's Book of Life:

> *And if anyone's name was not found written in the book of life,*
> *he was thrown into the lake of fire* (Revelation 20:15).

You might ask, "How can I get my name recorded in that book?"

> *But as many as received Him, to them He gave the right to*
> *become the children of God . . . who were born, not of blood nor*
> *of the will of the flesh nor of the will of man, but of God* (John
> 1:12–13).

When you receive Jesus Christ as your Savior, you are born again *(John 3)*. By that new birth, you leave the old bloodline of Adam and join the royal bloodline of Jesus Christ *(1 Peter 2:9)*. To be born into this new and eternally secure family of God, you must admit, "Lord, I'm not related to Your family; I'm not on my way to heaven—I'm on my way to hell. I'm in the wrong family, but I want to become a member of Your family. Please forgive my sin and make me Your child."

SPECIAL DONORS

I think the saddest word in **Nehemiah 7** is a word that appears two times—it is the word *some*:

> **Some *from among the heads of fathers' households gave to***
> **the work . . . Some *of the heads of fathers' households gave***
> **into the treasury of the work . . .** (Nehemiah 7:70–71).

How tragic that it did not read *all*. God appreciates those who willingly and graciously gave—and He knows them by name.

CITY OCCUPANTS

> **Now the city was large and spacious, but the people in it**
> **were few and the houses were not built** (Nehemiah 7:4).

Did you notice the problem Nehemiah revealed? Jerusalem was a large city with finished walls, but hardly any people were living on the inside. Nehemiah solved the problem in two ways.

Draftees

Now the leaders of the people lived in Jerusalem, but the rest of the people cast lots to bring one out of ten to live in Jerusalem, the holy city, while nine-tenths remained in the other cities (Nehemiah 11:1).

About one million people lived around Jerusalem. Since they could not all fit inside the walls, about 100,000 of them were drafted to move inside. Not every person would have wanted to uproot his family and relocate. Imagine the hassle and headaches, as well as the danger involved. Therefore, many were reluctant to move.

Volunteers

And the people blessed all the men who volunteered to live in Jerusalem (Nehemiah 11:2).

The Hebrew word for volunteer is the absolutely wonderful word *nadab*, and it means "to be impelled by an inner urge to stand; to be compelled to be courageous." It can be translated to read "to be noble."

These noble people stepped forward and said, "We will leave our secure countryside and our familiar surroundings. We will volunteer to uproot our families and move to the city of Jerusalem in order to help it grow and thrive." What better word is there to describe them than *noble*.

PRAYER WARRIORS

Among the noble ones, someone was known for his prayer life. He is given special mention as the credits continue to roll along:

[A]nd Mattaniah the son of Mica, the son of Zabdi, the son of Asaph, who was the leader in beginning the thanksgiving at prayer (Nehemiah 11:17a).

I love this entry in the long line of credits. Who was he? We don't really know. What did Mattaniah do? He was the Levite who started the prayer. He stood up at the appropriate time and began the prayer of thanksgiving. The only time he is ever mentioned in Scripture, this noble man is praying.

LESSONS ABOUT GIVING CREDIT

Most *of the Noble Things You Do Will Never Be Recognized on Earth*

Oftentimes, credit is *not* given where credit is due. Even if your effort is noticed, it may not be appreciated.

One pastor from Lubbock, Texas, has a humorous story which illustrates this point:

> When he began holding meetings in a nursing home as a young pastor, he noticed that one of the regulars who came would bring her television remote with her. Periodically, while he preached, she would scowl, aim that remote at him, and push the buttons. This went on for several months until he finally stopped one service, laughed good-naturedly, and said to her, "Ma'am, you can't turn me off with that." She just snapped back without blinking an eye, "I'm not trying to turn you off; I'm trying to change the channel!"

Perhaps we should all work on giving credit where credit is due. We need to discipline our minds to *notice* those who are serving and then *acknowledge* their contribution.

That ancient city and the contemporary Church have this in common: both would fail without noble volunteers giving their all for the King. Every church, missions organization, ministry, and Christian cause is moved forward, not by the few who are seen, but by an unseen labor force of staff members, prayer warriors, and volunteers throughout the ministry whose hearts have moved them to put forth their hands to the work. They do noble things which will probably never be fully calculated and rewarded on earth.

In the days of Nehemiah, the city of Jerusalem flourished because of the gatekeepers, guards, maintenance workers, groundskeepers, singers, priests, farmers, shepherds, special donors, and volunteers.

All *of the Noble Things You Do on Earth Will Be Recognized by God in Heaven*

For God is not unjust so as to forget your work and the love which you have shown toward His name, in having ministered and in still ministering to the saints (Hebrews 6:10).

People forget; people fail to say, "Thank you." People overlook you, but God never will. He always reads the credits. Better yet, He is in the process, at this very moment, of writing them.

So, let's roll the credits and read of noble ones who change the diapers and sweep the floors; answer telephones and pull weeds; arrange meetings and teach Bible lessons; prepare children's games and turn dials at the soundboard; clean the bathrooms and count the offering; practice the music and type the letters; pray through the "list" and visit guests; cook meals and offer rides; dust furniture and greet the family; translate sermons and duplicate CDs; park cars and prepare coffee; disciple teenagers and lead children to Christ; design brochures and stuff envelopes; crawl on the floor with toddlers and set up chairs in classrooms; wash the nursery linens and clean the dishes; recruit volunteers and thank the ones now serving; write curriculum and counsel at youth camp; listen to memory verses and stack chairs; unload equipment, load it back up, and then unload it all over again.

And remember, you are involved in *noble* work. Although it may be unrecognized on earth, one day it will be rewarded in heaven.

Ezra opened the book in the sight of all the people for he was standing above all the people; and when he opened it, all the people stood up. ⁶ Then Ezra blessed the LORD the great God. And all the people answered, "Amen, Amen!" while lifting up their hands; then they bowed low and worshiped the LORD with their faces to the ground. ⁷ Also Jeshua, Bani, Sherebiah, Jamin, Akkub, Shabbethai, Hodiah, Maaseiah, Kelita, Azariah, Jozabad, Hanan, Pelaiah, the Levites, explained the law to the people while the people remained in their place. ⁸ They read from the book, from the law of God, translating to give the sense so that they understood the reading. ⁹ Then Nehemiah, who was the governor, and Ezra the priest and scribe, and the Levites who taught the people said to all the people, "This day is holy to the LORD your God; do not mourn or weep." For all the people were weeping when they heard the words of the law. ¹⁰ Then he said to them, "Go, eat of the fat, drink of the sweet, and send portions to him who has nothing prepared; for this day is holy to our Lord. Do not be grieved, for the joy of the LORD is your strength." ¹¹ So the Levites calmed all the people, saying, "Be still, for the day is holy; do not be grieved." ¹² All the people went away to eat, to drink, to send portions and to celebrate a great festival, because they understood the words which had been made known to them.

—Nehemiah 8:5–12

CHAPTER TWELVE

LORD, SEND A ReBIBLE

Nehemiah 8

An anonymous writer observed a paradox of our generation:

We spend more but have less.

We buy more but enjoy it less.

We have bigger houses and smaller families.

We have more conveniences but less time.

We have more medicine but less wellbeing.

We read too little, watch TV too much, and pray too seldom.

We have multiplied our possessions but reduced our values.

We have tall men and short character, steep profits and shallow relationships.

We have two incomes but more divorce, fancier houses but broken homes.

We have added years to life, not life to years.

We have cleaned up the air but polluted the soul.

We have learned how to make a living but not a life.

One magazine article I read put it this way:

> There is much to celebrate. We now have, as average Americans, doubled our incomes and what money buys. We own twice as many cars per person and eat out two and a half times more often than our parents did. We have espresso

coffee, the World Wide Web, sport utility vehicles, and caller ID. New drugs are shrinking our tumors and lengthening our lives. Yet, at the same time, our divorce rate has doubled; teen suicide has tripled; violent crime has quadrupled; the number of babies born out of wedlock has sextupled; the number of cohabiting couples has increased from 500,000 twenty years ago to 4.2 million today.

Our economic good time has become dwarfed by our moral recession. One civic leader correctly assessed the problem when he said, "The accumulation of material goods is at an all-time high, but so is the number of people who feel an emptiness in their lives."

Pollster George Gallup, Jr., detected the same thing as he wrote, "One of the two dominant trends in society today is the search for spiritual moorings . . . surveys have documented the movement of people who are searching for meaning in life with a new intensity."

At the very time when the Church can step up to the microphone and announce that it has the answer in a personal Redeemer named Jesus Christ, it has, instead, *lost its voice.*

An author compiled a list of clippings and mailings sent out by a number of large churches, including one pastor's comment, "There is no fire and brimstone here. No Bible-thumping. Just practical, witty messages."

Another said, "Services at our church have an informal feeling. You won't hear people referred to as sinners. The goal is to make them feel welcome."

Here's another sample: "Our answer is God—but we slip Him in at the end, and even then, we don't get heavy. No ranting or raving. No fire, no brimstone. Our pastor doesn't even use the h-word. Call it Gospel Lite. It has the same salvation as the Old Time Religion but with a third less guilt."

And it continues: "The sermons are relevant, upbeat and, best of all, short. You won't hear a lot of preaching about sin. Preaching here doesn't sound like preaching. It is sophisticated, urbane, and friendly talk."

So the Church of our generation promises that the consumer will be satisfied rather than God being satisfied. If this is true, then God is no longer the *audience* of our worship; the audience has become "god." And the Church is feverishly trying to make this new god happy, comfortable, and satisfied. I heard of one church that has this motto: "It's all about you."

Church is *not* all about you, nor is it all about me—it is *all about the Triune God*. Our mandate from Jehovah God is not *self-centeredness* but *servanthood*. It is about selling ourselves to the mission of spreading the Gospel of Jesus Christ, the Son of God. It is about becoming passionately committed to the fact that man is sinful and on his way to hell.

The church that holds to the inerrant Word of God has the answer to our world's dilemma—it is the Gospel of Christ's death, burial, and resurrection. We should communicate that Gospel to our world as if we were throwing life preservers to drowning people. We are not to warm the water to make them more comfortable, nor should we offer lessons on how to float. We do not give self-help tips on how to manage life in the water. Absolutely not! We warn them they are going to drown if they do not come to the Savior. Many churches have lost the *moral courage* to communicate this life-saving message because it makes people uncomfortable.

The Church has also lost its *moral convictions*. In our generation, the materialism of the believer matches that of the world; the promiscuity and unfaithfulness of the believer mirrors the world; the self-centeredness of the believer almost *surpasses* that of the world. At the very time when the world needs the answer, the Church has lost the answer. The people of God today are in desperate need of revival.

So were the people of Jerusalem. They had finished the walls and were secure behind gates and gatekeepers. But there was a spiritual void in Jerusalem. They had everything *but* a right relationship with the God of Abraham, Isaac, and Jacob.

REVIVAL!

Nehemiah 8 will provide a blueprint and five necessary components for revival among God's people.

Please note that revival is *for believers only*—it does not apply to unbelievers. Why? According to *Ephesians 2:1*, an unbeliever is *dead in* [his] *trespasses and sins*. Therefore, if he is *dead*, he cannot be *revived*. A corpse has no life to revive. You revive a living person who is unconscious, a person in a coma, or someone who has been under water without oxygen for some time. You revive someone whose heart may have stopped beating when the possibility of resuscitation still exists. He can be revived because he is *not yet dead*.

This is true in the natural realm and also in the spiritual realm. "Revival" is warning the believer who is living like an unbeliever. His heart for God has stopped beating and the affections for God have subsided. He no longer breathes the air of fellowship with the Lord, and he is in need of resuscitation by the Father. David, a man after God's own heart, needed reviving. At one point he confessed:

> *Give me understanding, that I may observe Your law, and keep it with all my heart . . . and revive me in Your ways* (Psalm 119:34, 37).

A RENEWED APPETITE FOR SCRIPTURE

> **And all the people gathered as one man at the square which was in front of the Water Gate, and they asked Ezra the scribe to bring the book of the law of Moses which the LORD had given to Israel** (Nehemiah 8:1).

Did you notice the reappearance of Ezra, who by now was an old man? Years earlier, he had led a group back to Jerusalem, and they had rebuilt the temple. This man will now become the preacher as he reads, translates, and applies the text of the law for the people. The people of Jerusalem asked Ezra to bring the *book of the law* which God had given their nation. More than likely, this was a reference to the Pentateuch—the first five books of the Old Testament written by Moses. Their one unanimous cry was for *the book*. When a group of people, a family, an individual, or a church begin to *demand* the Scriptures, *revival* will not be far behind.

A native of India, writing to a friend about a revival they were having, wrote in English as he pronounced it in his native tongue: "We are having a great re-Bible here!" What a perfect slip of the pen. A revival is, indeed, when people are "re-Bibled." They hunger to hear, read, and learn the Word of God:

> **Then Ezra the priest brought the law before the assembly of men, women and all who could listen with understanding, on the first day of the seventh month. He read from it before the square which was in front of the Water Gate from early morning until midday, in the presence of men and women, those who could understand; and all the people**

were attentive to the book of the law. Ezra the scribe stood
at a wooden podium which they had made for the purpose.
And beside him stood [all the priests]. *Ezra opened the book*
in the sight of all the people for he was standing above all
the people; and when he opened it, all the people stood up
(Nehemiah 8:2–5).

They listened for six hours *standing up*, and this continued every day
for an entire week. Imagine that kind of hunger to hear the Word of God.

A RESPECTFUL ATTITUDE TOWARD GOD

Then Ezra blessed the LORD the great God (Nehemiah 8:6a).

That is another way of saying, "Ezra praised God for who God was—
the great, the awesome, the sovereign God." There is no revival if you have
a little god; a puny god who can be coerced and bribed; a petty god who,
like some divine genie, exists to do your will and fulfill your every wish; an
understandable god who is not majestic or transcendent; a weak god who can
barely keep up with his own creation.

Rather, revival comes to the hearts of those who encounter the Triune
God in all His splendor, holiness, and might. Yes, it comes to those who
acknowledge Him as the *Wonderful Counselor, the Mighty God, Eternal
Father, Prince of Peace* (Isaiah 9:6). Isaiah further described his great God:

> *Behold, the nations are like a drop from a bucket, and are*
> *regarded as a speck of dust on the scales; behold, He lifts up the*
> *islands like fine dust. To whom then will you liken God? Or what*
> *likeness will you compare with Him? It is He who sits above the*
> *circle of the earth, and its inhabitants are like grasshoppers, who*
> *stretches out the heavens like a curtain and spreads them out like*
> *a tent to dwell in. He it is who reduces rulers to nothing, who*
> *makes the judges of the earth meaningless* (Isaiah 40:15, 18,
> 22–23).

> *"To whom then will you liken Me that I would be his equal?"*
> *says the Holy One. Lift up your eyes on high and see who has*
> *created these stars, the One who leads forth their host by number,*
> *He calls them all by name; because of the greatness of His might*

and the strength of His power, not one of them is missing (Isaiah 40:25–26).

Do you not know? Have you not heard? The Everlasting God, the Lord, the Creator of the ends of the earth does not become weary or tired. His understanding is inscrutable. He gives strength to the weary, and to him who lacks might He increases power. Though youths grow weary and tired, and vigorous young men stumble badly, yet those who wait for the Lord will gain new strength; they will mount up with wings like eagles, they will run and not get tired, they will walk and not become weary (Isaiah 40:28–31).

Most of us run to verse 31 first and plead, "Dear Lord, I'm having a difficult time waiting, so please give me a shot of your 'strength tonic' for today, and help me fly like an eagle." However, the truth of this verse applies to someone who is waiting for the *kind of God* that Isaiah has just described. That person will receive strength. In fact, the word *wait* is a reference to contemplating or meditating on God's noble character, trusting in His eternal attributes, and relying on His great power and provision. The believer who is given power from God is the believer who has this perception of God. Believers who have a *small* God run out of gas; those who contemplate the awesome character of God, as described in *Isaiah 40* (as well as other passages) have strength for their daily walk.

And all the people answered, "Amen, Amen!" (Nehemiah 8:6*b*).

Amen, Amen or "so be it." The people were literally agreeing with Ezra's declaration and, in the process, they were getting a renewed vision of their awesome God:

[W]*hile lifting up their hands; then they bowed low and worshiped the LORD with their faces to the ground* (Nehemiah 8:6*c*).

The people in **Nehemiah 8** were moving toward a deeper respect for God. So much so that they knelt in contrition with their *faces to the ground.* Any renewed vision of the Almighty One is accompanied by a deep reverence for Him. Centuries later, the truth remains—revival comes from a *revived appetite* for the Scripture and a *reverential attitude* toward the Savior.

A RADICAL APPLICATION
OF BIBLICAL TRUTH

They read from the book, from the law of God, translating to give the sense so that they understood the reading (Nehemiah 8:8).

An interesting word appears several times in **Nehemiah 8**: *understand.* Why the repetition of this word? Why didn't the Jewish people understand the law when it was initially read to them? To answer these questions, let us attempt to read *Matthew 11:28–30*, taken from John Wycliffe's translation of the Greek language. It is the first English translation put into print, in the year 1382:

> *Alle ye that trauelen & ben chargid come to me & I schal fulfille you. Take ye my yok on you & lerne ye of me for I am mylde and meke in herte; and ye shulen finde rest to youre soulis for my yok is softe & my charge liyt.*

How did you do? If you tried hard enough and had it memorized, as well, you could probably make some sense of most of the words. However, because approximately six hundred years separate us from Wycliffe's world, many changes have taken place within the English language. Therefore, to gain a clearer understanding, the Bible has been translated into contemporary English. In the same way, between the time of Moses writing the book of the law and the time of Nehemiah, there was a span of *one thousand years.* Consider, also, that these people no longer spoke or understood Hebrew. They had Hebrew hearts but Babylonian ears. They simply needed to know what the words *meant.* But that was not all:

> ***Then on the second day the heads of fathers' households of all the people, the priests and the Levites were gathered to Ezra the scribe that they might gain insight into the words of the law*** (Nehemiah 8:13).

The word *insight* is translated from a Hebrew verb that means "to be wise or prudent." They wanted to understand the Word so they would have the insight or wisdom in how to apply the Word to their lives.

Another biblical illustration of this is found in Mark's Gospel, where the Lord broke the fish and loaves and fed over five thousand people. He showed His miraculous ability over the elements of nature by *creating* fish and bread. A few hours later, the disciples were terrified in a storm. Eventually, Jesus walked on the water to where they were, climbed into the boat, and commanded the storm to stop. Mark records,

> [A]*nd they were utterly astonished, for they had not gained any insight from the incident of the loaves* (Mark 6:51*b*–52*a*).

They had seen Christ's power demonstrated earlier, but they had not connected it with how they should live and act. In like manner, Nehemiah's generation desperately needed insight. They did not just need to hear the words, they needed to know how to *live* the words. There is a vast difference between biblical *input* and biblical *insight*. Insight brings about significant change, and significant change is always preceded by genuine sorrow.

APPROPRIATE SORROW OVER SIN

> **Then Nehemiah, who was the governor, and Ezra the priest and scribe, and the Levites who taught the people said to all the people, "This day is holy to the LORD your God; do not mourn or weep." For all the people were weeping when they heard the words of the law** (Nehemiah 8:9).

When the people rediscovered the truth of God's law, they began to mourn and weep as they realized how far they were from His standard. Perhaps we avoid the Word because of its supernatural ability to convict and challenge us to the very core of our motives and thoughts:

> *For the word of God is living and active and sharper than any two-edged sword, and piercing as far as the division of soul and spirit, of both joints and marrow, and able to judge the thoughts and intentions of the heart* (Hebrews 4:12).

The British playwright George Bernard Shaw once had a Bible. He sold it to auctioneers who, in turn, sold it for fifty dollars after Shaw's death in

1950. One of the selling points was an inscription on the flyleaf written by the playwright himself: *This book is a most undesirable possession . . . I must get rid of it. I really cannot bear it in my house!* He simply could not tolerate the stabs of guilt which pierced his heart by God's inspired Word.

Eventually Nehemiah stood and told the people to stop mourning and begin rejoicing. It was the day the Feast of Tabernacles was to begin:

> **Then he said to them, "Go, eat of the fat, drink of the sweet, and send portions to him who has nothing prepared; for this day is holy to our Lord. Do not be grieved, for the joy of the LORD is your strength." So the Levites calmed all the people, saying, "Be still, for the day is holy; do not be grieved." All the people went away to eat, to drink, to send portions and to celebrate a great festival, because they understood the words which had been made known to them** (Nehemiah 8:10–12).

AN ATTTITUDE OF OBEDIENCE AND JOY

A century ago, Matthew Henry wrote, "Holy joy will be oil to the wheels of our obedience." Notice how the people of Jerusalem obeyed:

> **They found written in the law how the LORD had commanded through Moses that the sons of Israel should live in booths during the feast of the seventh month. So they proclaimed and circulated a proclamation in all their cities and in Jerusalem, saying, "Go out to the hills, and bring olive branches and wild olive branches, myrtle branches, palm branches, and branches of other leafy trees, to make booths, as it is written." So the people went out and brought them and made booths for themselves, each on his roof, and in their courts and in the courts of the house of God, and in the square at the Water Gate and in the square at the Gate of Ephraim. The entire assembly of those who had returned from the captivity made booths and lived in them. The sons of Israel had indeed not done so from the days of Joshua the son of Nun to that day. And there was great rejoicing** (Nehemiah 8:14–17).

God said for them to build little shanties and lean-to shacks out of branches so they could remember their journey in the wilderness. This custom did not make much sense to the modern Jew. They *needed* to continue rebuilding their own homes inside the newly constructed city walls. But God's Word said, "Build booths using leafy trees." They unhesitatingly responded, "We'll build booths, just as the Word commanded." The end result was great rejoicing. *Insight led to obedience, and obedience led to joy.*

THE EVIDENCES OF TRUE REVIVAL

Replacing Cop-Outs with Confession

The following is a great example of *using* errors instead of admitting error:

> In 1992, the Texas educational bureaucracy reviewed and approved a new set of history textbooks for the public school system. A group of parents, concerned about the information their children were coming home with conducted their own review. They found 231 errors. The textbook reported Napoleon actually winning the battle of Waterloo, President Truman dropping the atom bomb on Korea, and General Douglas MacArthur (instead of Senator Joe McCarthy) leading the anti-Communist campaign in the 1950s. When called to account for these errors, the Texas officials studied the texts again. They found more than the 231 errors the parents had first found; then the parents found more, until the tally eventually stood at 5,200 mistakes in texts published by Prentice-Hall, Houghton Mifflin, and Rinehart and Winston. How did the publishers react to this mess? A spokesperson argued that, "Except for the errors, these were the finest textbooks they had ever seen."

The believer who wants true revival throws away the list of favorite excuses for his or her sin. Confession *replaces* excuses.

Replacing Compromise with Courage

You might say, "I've confessed, tried, and failed so many times—revival just doesn't last." Someone made this comment to evangelist Billy Sunday in the early 1900s and tried to make the point that since personal revival wasn't a permanent end-all to temptation, sin, and failure, revival wasn't important. Billy Sunday replied with his characteristic humor, "A bath doesn't last either, but it's good to have one occasionally." It isn't easy—you have to muster up courage for each new day. If you want fellowship with the Father, you'll need reviving every day, as well.

Replacing Complacency with Commitment

According to the Apostle Paul, we are compared to earthen vessels in which the Father has chosen to put His priceless treasure *(2 Corinthians 4:7)*. Since we are *cracked* pots, we must stay close to the source of divine strength and fellowship in order to enjoy His presence day by day, moment by moment. The only way to keep a cracked pot filled with water is to keep it under the faucet.

Are *you* in need of revival? If so, authentic renewal will come when you:

- approach God with due respect and adoration;
- apply what you learn;
- repent, repent, and *repent*;
- obey.

While you're at it, make sure you stay under the faucet of God's Word . . . and keep it flowing.

Now on the twenty-fourth day of this month the sons of Israel assembled with fasting, in sackcloth and with dirt upon them. ²The descendants of Israel separated themselves from all foreigners, and stood and confessed their sins and the iniquities of their fathers. ³While they stood in their place, they read from the book of the law of the LORD their God for a fourth of the day; and for another fourth they confessed and worshiped the LORD their God. ⁴Now on the Levites' platform stood Jeshua, Bani, Kadmiel, Shebaniah, Bunni, Sherebiah, Bani, and Chenani, and they cried with a loud voice to the LORD their God.

—Nehemiah 9:1–4

CHAPTER THIRTEEN

TRUE CONFESSION

Nehemiah 9

In an article entitled "Playing Charades," Dr. Perry Buffington released his findings on the lack of transparency in certain situations. He found that the average person puts on airs, acting differently than they feel inwardly, in certain situations.

> **When entering an automobile showroom**
>
> Most people try to hide their true emotions in an attempt to protect themselves from aggressive salesmen. They tend to act unaffected by what they see, even though their heart may be racing.

> **When entering the lobby of an upscale hotel**
>
> In this instance, people try to exude an air of importance in an attempt to come across as someone comfortable and at home in lavish surroundings.

> **When entering a church**
>
> They pretend they have nothing to hide from God and fellow worshippers. They put on a sacred air in their conversations even though they are uncomfortable with who they know they truly are on the inside.

This article proposes that we have become skilled at *acting* authentic, *faking* our fellowship with God, *impersonating* the saints, and *simulating* spirituality. We are far too concerned with being seen as people who seem to have it all together.

For example, take the story of a rather single-minded, self-confident businessman who always seemed on top of it. Even though he worked seventy- and eighty-hour weeks, he was an organized man. He had a cottage built on a lake to use as a weekend retreat. To make his plan even more efficient, he learned how to fly and kept another car for weekend transport at the airfield nearest the lake. That plan wasn't quite efficient enough, so he fine-tuned his plane, fitting it with pontoons so he could land on the lake and actually taxi right up to his newly constructed pier.

On his first trip he flew, by force of habit, straight to the rural airport and started his descent. "What are you doing?" His wife suddenly screamed, "There aren't any wheels on this plane!" There was just enough time to pull up before touching down. Somewhat shaken, he flew to the lake and made a perfect landing. As the plane drifted to a stop at the pier, he turned to his wife and said, "I'm sorry, dear. I did know what I was doing; I just lost my thought for a moment there. I should have planned more carefully and built in reminders about the change in flight plans. It won't happen again." Then, he opened his door and hopped confidently out of the plane and directly into the lake!

The moral of the story is never let anybody see you for who you really are—including your spouse. You must always have your life "under control." Hopefully, this does *not* characterize your life because this is a self-centered, naturally depraved, totally carnal philosophy of life which inhibits communion with the Father and with others.

Has it ever occurred to you that a great word to describe Christianity is *exposure*? You became a Christian after being *exposed* as a sinner. You grow as a Christian after being *exposed* as an infant, needing the Word. You are to confess sin as others, including the Holy Spirit, *expose* it in your life. Without this spiritual exposure, we would never achieve growth and revival.

We are encouraged by both our culture and our sinful nature to cover up, pretend, and put on airs. This is one of the chief obstacles to revival in our personal lives. Above all, we are told *never* to expose our true selves to anyone—especially God. This will only result in feeling guilty. Then suddenly our lives intersect with the living Word of God which, according to *Hebrews 4:12*, is powerful and sharper than any two-edged sword. We read it and it penetrates our thoughts, as well as our intentions. There is no room for charades. The Word of God opens the curtain, takes off our masks, exposes our inward thoughts and motives, and then demands radical change.

In our study of chapter eight, we observed the Jewish people hearing, for the first time in their lives, the law of Moses. They began to weep and mourn. There was no need or attempt to fake anything. The law of God's Word was a plumb line—as they held it up to themselves, they realized how crooked they were, and they grieved over their condition.

TRUE CONFESSION OBSERVED

It was as true then as it is today: genuine confession comes from an encounter with God's Word, exposing us for who we truly are. Confession begins when you discover the truth of Scripture and passionately apply it to your life. In **Nehemiah 8**, that process had already begun. Chapter nine gives us a *model of confession*. The vital ingredients of the revival process are revealed. If you want to stop pretending and if you want to be transparent, these entries in Nehemiah's memoirs will show you how.

Years ago, I received a request from a neighbor whose six-year-old son often played with our six-year-old daughter. It seemed his class was having a year-end party and part of the festivities included a show-and-tell time. When the boy's mom asked him what he wanted to take to school for show-and-tell, he thought a moment and then said, "I want to take Charity!" So his mom was asking for permission. I had never heard of a *person* being taken for show-and-tell, but it certainly was a nice compliment to our daughter. Charity did accompany him, and they both thought it was great—especially the ice cream and cake.

The people of Israel are God's show-and-tell for us; they are a true model of confession. Let's observe and follow their example.

CHARACTERISTICS OF TRUE CONFESSION
A Humble Approach to God's Presence

Something very interesting took place which was not a part of the Jewish calendar:

> ***Now on the twenty-fourth day of this month the sons of Israel assembled with fasting, in sackcloth and with dirt upon them*** (Nehemiah 9:1).

This action catches my attention because it was not prescribed or commanded by Nehemiah or Ezra. Rather, it was the natural outpouring of true brokenness over sin. Did you notice what the people were wearing? Not the latest, most up-to-date fashions but *sackcloth* and *ashes*. All pretenses and saintly masquerades were gone. In fact, the dirt was a way of exposing and admitting their soiled hearts before God and each other. This was, undoubtedly, the most humble way they could approach Almighty God.

An Honest Admission of Personal Sinfulness

The descendants of Israel separated themselves from all foreigners, and stood and confessed their sins and the iniquities of their fathers (Nehemiah 9:2).

True confession is evidenced when you do not blame your sinfulness on the sin of your parents. Even if they are guilty, *you* are responsible for *your own choice* to sin.

> **While they stood in their place, they read from the book of the law of the LORD their God for a fourth of the day** [three hours]**; and for another fourth** [three hours] **they confessed and worshiped the LORD their God** (Nehemiah 9:3).

A few years ago, James Montgomery Boice was asked if he believed America was experiencing revival. He responded by writing:

> Whenever I have been asked that question, my answer has always been, "No." The reason I say no is quite simple—there is not a national consciousness of sin. In fact, there is hardly any consciousness of sin. When revival sweeps over a people, the first evidence is a profound awareness of sin and sorrow for it.

In other words, confession includes admission, and admission is an evidence of revival.

G. K. Chesterton, a famous philosopher and theologian, once read a series of articles entitled "What's Wrong with the World?" According to the story "The Lostness of Humankind," told by Ravi Zacharias on *Preaching Today*, Chesterton sent a short letter to the editor which read:

> Dear Sir:

> Regarding your article, "What's Wrong with the World?"—I am!

Yours truly,
G. K. Chesterton.

Writing to *believers*, the Apostle John wrote,

If we say that we have no sin, we are deceiving ourselves and the truth is not in us. If we say that we have not sinned, we make Him a liar and His word is not in us (1 John 1:8, 10).

Squeezed between verses 8 and 10 is the following requirement for revival: *If we confess our sins . . .* (1 John 1:9*a*). Confess is the Greek word *homologeo* which means "to say the same thing about our actions as God says." God says it is sin, and we agree, "Yes Lord, it is, indeed, sin." Now, the promise follows:

He is faithful and righteous to forgive us our sins and to cleanse us from all unrighteousness (1 John 1:9*b*).

The most miserable person on planet Earth is a believer living *in sin*. He cannot fully enjoy his sin because of his guilty conscience and he can no longer enjoy fellowship with God.

That reminds me of the preacher who called in sick one Sunday morning and had one of his associates preach for him, but he actually went golfing. There he was out golfing on Sunday morning; the angels were watching. So was the Lord. The Lord said to His angels, "I'm going to make that disobedient pastor absolutely miserable."

About that time, the preacher teed up his ball and hit it perfectly onto the green and it rolled right into the cup. A hole in one!

The angels said, "Lord, how is *that* going to make him miserable?"

The Lord replied, "Who can he tell?"

Hear now from the diary of a believer who was caught in the guilt of sin and the misery of refusing to confess. David writes,

When I kept silent about my sin, my body wasted away through my groaning all day long. For day and night Your hand was heavy upon me; my vitality was drained away as with the fever heat of summer. I acknowledged my sin to You, and my iniquity I did not hide; I said, "I will confess my transgressions to the LORD"; and You forgave the guilt of my sin (Psalm 32:3–5).

This is honest, open admission of sin! This is the beginning of personal revival. In **Nehemiah 9**, we observe the people of Jerusalem passionately admitting their sin before the Lord:

> **And they cried with a loud voice to the LORD their God** (Nehemiah 9:4*b*).

An Honorable Acknowledgement of God's Greatness

> **"O may Your glorious name be blessed and exalted above all blessing and praise! You alone are the LORD"** (Nehemiah 9:5*b*–6*a*).

This is putting God in His proper place. When we pray like this, we find it a lot harder to pray to Him as if He is a doting grandfather or a genie in a bottle. This perspective enables us to see Him as He truly is—the God who reigns in the heavens, majestic in splendor, and sovereign in all things. This illustrates the way the Lord taught His disciples to pray. He encouraged them to begin praying by acknowledging the greatness of God: *"Our Father, who is in heaven"* (Matthew 6:9). So, when you begin your prayer with the words "Heavenly Father," you are actually saying, "Majestic, Holy, Sovereign, Creator, Eternal Father." True prayer does not *trivialize* God, it pays *tribute* to Him.

Now notice how the prayer of Ezra in this chapter does exactly that. He acknowledges the greatness, goodness, and sovereign power of God.

OBSERVING THE GREATNESS OF GOD

Let's go back in time, slip into some of that sackcloth along with the people of Jerusalem, and enter into the prayer of Ezra.

> ➢ **His superb creation of the universe**
>
> **"O may Your glorious name be blessed and exalted above all blessing and praise! You alone are the LORD. You have made the heavens, the heaven of heavens with all their host, the earth and all that is on it, the seas and all that is in them. You give life to all of them and the heavenly host bows down before You"** (Nehemiah 9:5*b*–6).

> ➢ **His sovereign calling of Abraham**

"You are the LORD God, who chose Abram and brought him out from Ur of the Chaldees, and gave him the name Abraham. You found his heart faithful before You, and made a covenant with him to give him the land of the Canaanite, of the Hittite and the Amorite, of the Perizzite, the Jebusite and the Girgashite—to give it to his descendants. And You have fulfilled Your promise, for You are righteous" (Nehemiah 9:7–8).

➤ **His supernatural conquest over Egypt**

"You saw the affliction of our fathers in Egypt, and heard their cry by the Red Sea. Then You performed signs and wonders against Pharaoh, against all his servants and all the people of his land; for You knew that they acted arrogantly toward them, and made a name for Yourself as it is this day. You divided the sea before them, so they passed through the midst of the sea on dry ground; and their pursuers You hurled into the depths, like a stone into raging waters. And with a pillar of cloud You led them by day, and with a pillar of fire by night to light for them the way in which they were to go" (Nehemiah 9:9–12).

➤ **His scriptural commands from Mount Sinai**

"Then You came down on Mount Sinai, and spoke with them from heaven; You gave them just ordinances and true laws, good statutes and commandments. So You made known to them Thy holy sabbath, and laid down for them commandments, statutes and law, through Your servant Moses. You provided bread from heaven for them for their hunger, You brought forth water from a rock for them for their thirst, and You told them to enter in order to possess the land which You swore to give them. But they, our fathers, acted arrogantly; they became stubborn and would not listen to Your commandments. They refused to listen, and did not remember Your wondrous deeds which You had performed among them; so they became stubborn and

appointed a leader to return to their slavery in Egypt. But You are a God of forgiveness, gracious and compassionate, slow to anger and abounding in lovingkindness; and You did not forsake them. Even when they made for themselves a calf of molten metal and said, 'This is your God Who brought you up from Egypt,' and committed great blasphemies" (Nehemiah 9:13–18).

➢ **His satisfying covenant with Israel**

"You, in Your great compassion, did not forsake them in the wilderness; the pillar of cloud did not leave them by day, to guide them on their way, nor the pillar of fire by night, to light for them the way in which they were to go. You gave Your good Spirit to instruct them, Your manna You did not withhold from their mouth, and You gave them water for their thirst. Indeed, forty years You provided for them in the wilderness and they were not in want; their clothes did not wear out, nor did their feet swell. You also gave them kingdoms and peoples, and allotted them to them as a boundary. They took possession of the land of Sihon the king of Heshbon and the land of Og the king of Bashan. You made their sons numerous as the stars of heaven, and You brought them into the land which You had told their fathers to enter and possess. So their sons entered and possessed the land. And You subdued before them the inhabitants of the land, the Canaanites, and You gave them into their hand, with their kings and the peoples of the land, to do with them as they desired. They captured fortified cities and a fertile land. They took possession of houses full of every good thing, hewn cisterns, vineyards, olive groves, fruit trees in abundance. So they ate, were filled and grew fat, and reveled in Your great goodness" (Nehemiah 9:19–25).

➢ **His steadfast compassion towards His people**

"But they became disobedient and rebelled against You, and cast Your law behind their backs and killed Your prophets

who had admonished them so that they might return to You, and they committed great blasphemies. Therefore You delivered them into the hand of their oppressors who oppressed them, but when they cried to You in the time of their distress, You heard from heaven, and according to Your great compassion You gave them deliverers who delivered them from the hand of their oppressors. But as soon as they had rest, they did evil again before You; therefore You abandoned them to the hand of their enemies, so that they ruled over them. When they cried again to You, You heard from heaven, and many times You rescued them according to Your compassion, and admonished them in order to turn them back to Your law. Yet they acted arrogantly and did not listen to Your commandments but sinned against Your ordinances, by which if a man observes them he shall live. And they turned a stubborn shoulder and stiffened their neck, and would not listen. However, You bore with them for many years, and admonished them by Your Spirit through Your prophets, yet they would not give ear. Therefore You gave them into the hand of the peoples of the lands. Nevertheless, in Your great compassion You did not make an end of them or forsake them, for You are a gracious and compassionate God. Now therefore, our God, the great, the mighty, and the awesome God, who keeps covenant and lovingkindness, do not let all the hardship seem insignificant before You, which has come upon us, our kings, our princes, our priests, our prophets, our fathers and on all Your people, from the days of the kings of Assyria to this day. However, You are just in all that has come upon us; for You have dealt faithfully, but we have acted wickedly. For our kings, our leaders, our priests and our fathers have not kept Your law or paid attention to Your commandments and Your admonitions with which You have admonished them. But they, in their own kingdom, with Your great goodness which You gave them, with the broad and rich land which You set before them, did not serve You or turn from their evil deeds. Behold, we are slaves today, and as to the land which You gave to our fathers to eat of its fruit and its bounty, behold, we are slaves on it. Its abundant produce is for the kings whom You have set over us because of our sins; they also rule over our bodies and over our cattle as they please, so we are in great distress. Now because of all this we are making an agreement in writing; and on the sealed document are the names of our leaders, our Levites and our priests" (Nehemiah 9:26–38).

THE IMPORTANCE OF TRUE CONFESSION

What a summary! The people admitted to blasphemy, stubbornness, arrogance, refusing to listen to the Scriptures, stiffening their necks, closing their ears, becoming disobedient, rebellious, scorning the law, refusing to pay attention to the law and ordinances of God, refusing to serve Him, and refusing to repent before Him.

There are no disguises here—no masks. In this model of confession, sin is exposed and God is begged to forgive and pour out His grace and mercy.

An Awareness of Personal Corruption and Guilt

The average Christian is in need of revival because we learn to live with as much sin as our consciences will allow. We sugarcoat our selfishness, rationalize our rebellion, and excuse our failure to execute obedience to God. We *manage* our sin—we do not *confess* our sin. We have forgotten how heartbreaking and how grievous sin in the life of a believer is to our heavenly Father.

A pastor wrote a rather interesting article in a minister's journal; it dealt with a problem in the bathroom of a middle school in Oregon. Girls were setting the precedent of pressing their lips to the mirrors after applying lipstick, leaving dozens of messy lip prints all over the glass.

When the principal declared that something must be done, she devised a rather ingenious plan and told the custodian exactly what to do. After summoning the girls and the custodian to the bathroom, the principal explained that the lip prints were causing a major problem for the custodian, and instructed the girls to stop the nasty practice that wasted his valuable time.

Of course, the girls were oblivious to this request and were irritated at having to meet with the principal—they didn't even try to hide it. Not being deterred, the principal continued with her scheme and asked the custodian to show them how he had been cleaning the mirrors each day after school.

He promptly took out his long-handled brush, dipped it into one of the nearby toilets, and scrubbed the mirrors with the brush. The girls' mouths dropped open in shock. Not surprisingly, since that demonstration, the lip prints have never reappeared!

Confession is the fresh realization that sin is corruption and filth. You shudder to think what you have been kissing up to; the justification stops, the rationalizing stops, the believer mourns, laments, and pleads to be rescued from sin's allurement because it no longer looks appealing. Now, if that was all confession was—an awareness of corruption—we would be led to the point of despair.

A Reminder of God's Character and Grace

"But You are a God of forgiveness, gracious and compassionate, slow to anger and abounding in lovingkindness" (Nehemiah 9:17*b*).

"And many times You rescued them according to Your compassion" (Nehemiah 9:28*b*).

"However, You bore with them for many years" (Nehemiah 9:30*a*).

"However, You are just in all that has come upon us; for You have dealt faithfully, but we have acted wickedly" (Nehemiah 9:33).

Anyone in tune with God is often overwhelmed by his own guilt and by God's amazing grace.

Revival *commences* with the content of Scripture *(chapter 8)*; it *continues* with the confession of sin *(chapter 9)*; it will be *confirmed* by the commitment of servanthood. This commitment will be the next entry as Nehemiah journals his amazing pilgrimage toward the blessing of God.

And on that day they offered great sacrifices and rejoiced because God had given them great joy, even the women and children rejoiced, so that the joy of Jerusalem was heard from afar.

—Nehemiah 12:43

CHAPTER FOURTEEN

DECLARATION OF DEPENDENCE

Nehemiah 10–12

O n July 4, we celebrate the birth of our country in 1776. A document declaring our independence from Great Britain was drawn up and voted on July 2 in the city of Philadelphia, although it was dated July 4. It would be another month before those famous signatures would be appended to that historic paper marking the birth of a new nation under God, the closing words of which solemnly declare:

> With a firm reliance on the protection of divine Providence, we mutually pledge to each other our lives, our fortunes, and our sacred honor.

The fifty-six men who signed the document understood it was more than bold rhetoric. If the struggle for independence was successful, the best they could expect would be years of personal hardship and strife. The Declaration of Independence was, in actuality, a declaration of *dependence* upon each other and the providence of God.

Through the personal diary of Nehemiah, we have watched revival come to the nation of Israel. It began with a hunger for the Word of God and a willingness to obey it. They were a people who were literally *reBibled*, for any *revival* is nothing short of people living out the principles and truths of God's Holy Word. Their renewal also involved true confession and deep mourning over their sin.

Based on our observation of Israel during this time, we could define "revival" as:

1. A movement of God's Spirit in the believer's life which produces both private confession of sin and public obedience to the Scriptures.

2. Outward behavior marked with God's pleasure as the highest priority—a priority that will undeniably impact personal relationships, financial dealings, and lifestyle decisions.

Revival is, therefore, not a once-and-done event. True revival could be likened to remodeling your kitchen. It takes longer than you planned, makes a bigger mess than you ever thought possible, and costs more than you initially calculated. Revival is incredibly inconvenient. It will upend one's entire life.

You cannot *plan* for revival, you can only *pray* for it. You cannot orchestrate it or announce that it is going to happen in a series of meetings in the third week of June. All you can do is ask God for it to happen in your life—for Him to awaken you to your sin and to the authority and wonder of His Word and to blow on the smoldering embers of your heart so that they burst into flaming affection for Him once again. Pray as David prayed:

Will You not Yourself revive us again? (Psalm 85:6).

Revival is not so much about *emotion* as it is about *action*. If anything, the emotion of revival is soon followed by the action of revival.

Nehemiah 10 reveals the action of the Jewish people—action that confirmed the presence of true revival.

EVIDENCES OF TRUE REVIVAL

When You Rededicate Your Feet to Follow after God's Precepts

Now on the sealed document were the names of: Nehemiah the governor, the son of Hacaliah . . . Now the rest of the people, the priests, the Levites, the gatekeepers, the singers, the temple servants and all those who had separated themselves from the peoples of the lands to the law of God, their wives, their sons and their daughters, all those who had knowledge and understanding, are joining with their kinsmen, their nobles, and are taking on themselves a curse

*and an oath to walk in God's law, which was given through
Moses, God's servant, and to keep and to observe all the
commandments of GOD our Lord, and His ordinances and
His statutes* (Nehemiah 10:1, 28, 29).

The people had only recently blown the dust off the book and heard it
read to them for the first time in their entire lives. But after the first hearing,
they knew that if it was indeed God's book, it was binding and authoritative
over their lives. It was not an optional guide—it was the will of God.

Is there a New Testament counterpoint for this same response? Yes. Paul
commanded,

Let the word of Christ richly dwell within you, with all wisdom
(Colossians 3:16a).

The word *dwell* can be translated "take up residence." In other words,
Paul is exhorting the believer to let the Word of God make a home in your
heart. Consequently, a revival occurs in the believer's life when he puts out
the welcome mat for the Word.

Richly involves a word that could be rendered "extravagantly." Said differently, it knows no boundaries. A believer doesn't say to the Word, "Come
into my life, but stay over there in the corner. Don't go into the family room.
Don't go into the bedroom. Don't go anywhere except to church with me on
Sunday. And whatever you do, don't go to work with me! Just stay here in your
designated place, until I *need* You!" No, this verse urges the believer to let the
Word have *full reign* in every compartment, department, and segment of life.

The people in Nehemiah's day were saying nothing short of this: "We
will allow the *Scriptures* to determine everything about our lifestyle":

[We will] *walk in God's law . . .* [We will] *observe all the
commandments of GOD our Lord and His ordinances and
His statutes* (Nehemiah 10:29b).

When You Rededicate Your Family
and Personal Lifestyle to Biblical Purity

[A]*nd that we will not give our daughters to the peoples of the
land or take their daughters for our sons* (Nehemiah 10:30).

Our culture today is obviously very different from Nehemiah's. Parents don't choose their children's spouses . . . although, the older my children get, the more attractive that idea becomes to me. Even though vast differences exist culturally, a timeless principle that transcends cultures and generations is this: "We will accept the importance of godly relationships." The New Testament counter-passage says *do not be bound together with unbelievers* (2 Corinthians 6:14). In the King James Version, this is translated *be ye not unequally yoked together with unbelievers.* In Paul's day the concept of an unequal yoke was used in relation to marriage. Do not be yoked together with unbelievers would simply mean do not marry an unbeliever.

You might already be married to an unbeliever. Paul makes it very clear in *1 Corinthians 7* that the believing spouse is not to send away the unbeliever in an effort to start over and marry a believer. God's Word counsels the believer in a case like this to remain with the unbelieving spouse and become a living testimony to the saving grace of God. That testimony is called by Paul a sanctifying presence in the home for the sake of the children and, hopefully, for their salvation.

Someone might ask, "Why would a believer be told not to marry an unbeliever?" Paul anticipates that question and continues by asking a few questions of his own:

> [W]*hat has a believer in common with an unbeliever? Or what agreement has the temple of God with idols? For we are the temple of the living God; just as God said, "I will dwell in them and walk among them; and I will be their God, and they shall be My people. Therefore, come out from their midst and be separate," says the Lord* (2 Corinthians 6:15–17).

You could apply this principle of separation to the business world as well by not engaging in partnerships with unbelievers.

Now, obviously, each situation calls for wisdom and biblical application. We live in a world with unbelievers, and we do business with unbelievers every day. In fact, even in the world of relationships, if you do not have friendships with unbelievers, how will you ever reach them for Christ? God intends for us to be salt and light. The point is that you need to ask God how and where to draw the line in personal and business relationships.

A financial planner called me for counsel. A few months earlier, he had been approached by a religious cult to manage their finances. He was troubled in knowing that by helping them financially, he would indirectly be aiding them in spreading their false doctrine. So he turned them down. In doing so, he walked away from what could have been great financial gain. I admire him for his courage and conviction.

I wonder how many business owners sell alcoholic beverages and then teach, "Your body is God's temple," in Sunday school. How many business owners would have the courage to place Bibles in their waiting rooms and play Christian music over their intercom system?

One of the reasons revival has been hindered in our generation is because we, as believers, no longer *agonize* over the issues of godly distinction. We have condemned convictions of holiness as legalism and have become strangely compatible with the world and its lifestyle. Can you name at least five things you do that nearly everyone else around you does not do? Can you think of five things *you* do not do that, if asked for the reason, the answer would be, "Because I am a follower of Christ and do not believe it would please Him"?

Talk about sounding strange. Some may say, or at least think, *You have got to be kidding. What are you—some sort of fanatic?* The answer is a resounding, "Yes!" I certainly *should* be a fanatic for Christ and His precepts.

Consider the New Testament call, *"Come out from their midst and be separate"* (2 Corinthians 6:17). Can you answer how that verse is applied in your own life? Do you know how your life is different from an unbeliever? Do you know how to apply godly separation in your walk with Christ? My friend, if you do not know at least five ways that your life is different from your unbelieving neighbor, you are probably in need of revival.

In his commentary on Nehemiah entitled *Hand Me Another Brick*, Charles Swindoll quotes Keith Miller:

> It has never ceased to amaze me that we Christians have developed a kind of selective vision which allows us to be deeply and sincerely involved in worship and church activities, and yet almost totally pagan in the day in, day out guts of our business lives and never even realize it.

Swindoll goes on to add a word of personal commitment and challenge:

> We won't care if anyone else in the world lives by [godly standards]. We will live by them. We won't shrug our shoulders, yawn, and say, "It doesn't matter," when our kids want to mix

and mingle with the crowd. Our homes will be distinct. Our philosophy of life will not be like that of those who live outside the walls of the Church. This is our promise to You, O God.

For those who refuse to live distinctly for Christ—those who live as close to the edge as they possibly can—the dangers of spiritual erosion and corruption are prowling ever closer. When a believer decides to set aside the Word of God as his manual for living, he sets in motion the laws of spiritual compromise and, perhaps, terrible consequences.

A military pilot told me about his experiences learning how to fly a high-powered jet. At one stage of his training, he was flying at night to learn to depend on his instrument panel. The instructor suddenly ordered him to close his eyes and fly entirely by his instincts. So he closed his eyes and began to pilot the plane according to his "feelings." After several minutes, the instructor asked him, "How do you think you're doing?"

To which he responded, "We're doing great!"

The instructor said, "Open your eyes."

When he did, he discovered that they were actually flying upside down, heading straight toward the ground. He had become another victim of vertigo, a condition that without the aid of sight distorts the reality of position and balance.

In a similar way, it is possible for the believer to become affected with worldly vertigo and say, "I'm doing great," while in reality he is heading for a terrible crash. Revival is when we pull out of our collision course by refusing to fly by our own instincts and, once again, obey the instrument panel of God's Word.

When You Rededicate Your Faith in God's Providence

As for the peoples of the land who bring wares or any grain on the sabbath day to sell, we will not buy from them on the sabbath or a holy day; and we will forego the crops the seventh year and the exaction of every debt (Nehemiah 10:31).

Imagine, they just signed their names and effectively promised not to do as the world does in the following ways:

- We will not do business on the Sabbath.
- We will not plant crops in the seventh year.
- We will forgive any debt against us by a fellow Jew.

These were unique commitments to the nation of Israel. Paul made it clear in *Galatians 4* that believers are not bound to special days or festivals.

Every day of the week is holy to the New Testament Christian. But the principle is timeless. Jews were to trust God to provide for them. Can you imagine not planting crops every seventh year? Can you imagine wiping every loan off your books that others owed you? Do you think you would be inclined to loan anyone anything during the *sixth* year? How about in December of the sixth year? This was God's built-in curriculum on faith. And every Israelite had to enroll. The name of the course was *Trust 101*. It could not be audited or skipped. Trusting God for provision in these unique ways was a reminder that ultimately He was *the* Provider. Anybody who trusted God like that certainly had a thorough dose of true revival.

When You Rededicate Your Finances to Acknowledge God's Priorities

In chapters 10 and 12, as the walls are dedicated and the choirs sing with great joy, the people also sign a declaration that they will devote whatever is necessary to maintain the house of worship. You could call it a Declaration of *Dependence*.

> *We also placed ourselves under obligation to contribute yearly one third of a shekel for the service of the house of our God: for the showbread, for the continual grain offering, for the continual burnt offering, the sabbaths, the new moon, for the appointed times, for the holy things and for the sin offerings to make atonement for Israel, and all the work of the house of our God. Likewise we cast lots for the supply of wood among the priests, the Levites and the people so that they might bring it to the house of our God, according to our fathers' households, at fixed times annually, to burn on the altar of the LORD our God, as it is written in the law; . . . thus we will not neglect the house of our God* (Nehemiah 10:32–34, 39).

I agree with Warren Wiersbe who said that true revival will always reveal itself in the way we support God's work, beginning in our own local church. Frankly, I am convinced that the most sensitive nerve in a person's body is the nerve that runs from his heart to his back pocket. What people do with their money profoundly reveals their soul's condition. Jesus Christ summed up this principle when He said,

"[F]or where your treasure is, there your heart will be also" (Matthew 6:21).

To put this in the language of our day, "We don't put our money where our mouth is, we put our money where our *heart* is."

I read with interest and sadness an article by the late Larry Burkett in *Christianity Today* magazine. Burkett's ministry (Christian financial training) receives tens of thousands of calls per year. In this article, Burkett said that the profile of the average caller for financial advice is someone in their early forties, with two children and an annual household income of $40,000. They have a $125,000 mortgage on their home; they owe $20,000 in automobile loans and $6,000 in educational loans and carry $7,000 to $10,000 on their credit cards. The average believer is in desperate need of "plastic surgery"—not the physical kind.

You could safely say that revival is a surrender of your *soul*, a surrender of your *wallet*, a surrender of your *family*, a surrender of your *will* and, yes, a surrender of your *all* to your great, awesome, holy, and gracious God—who has lavished upon you His wonderful love. As Winston Churchill once poignantly stated, "We make a living by what we get, but we make a life by what we give."

THE RESULTS OF REVIVAL

When true revival comes, believers will **be unable to remain selfish** and **be unable to keep silent** about their Lord.

Authentic revival will have one primary, undeniable outcome: **joy**! The choirs are proceeding along the wall. The declaration has been signed, and the people have vowed to keep their God and their worship of Him their highest priority. I love Nehemiah's insertion in his diary that reveals a volume of praise:

> **[A]nd on that day they offered great sacrifices and rejoiced because God had given them great joy, even the women and children rejoiced, so that the joy of Jerusalem was heard from afar** (Nehemiah 12:43).

Imagine that! The joy of Jerusalem was heard from afar. The people had literally returned to *joy*—from the young to the elderly, all were affected by it. Not only had the walls, gates, bricks, and mortar been restored, but so had their joy.

Likewise, when David returned to the heart of God, his longing was for that same quality which he had forfeited years earlier. He longed for it and pleaded for it as he prayed, *"Restore to me the joy of Your salvation"* (Psalm

51:12*a*). Revived believers cannot stay sorrowful, silent, or selfish because their hearts are filled with affection for God and His people. Indeed, His will and His Word are no longer optional but are our joyful obligation.

Gipsy Smith, a well-known English evangelist from the previous generation, was approached by a man and asked how to begin to pray for revival in this country. Gipsy asked him, "Do you have a place where you can go to pray?"

"Yes," was the reply.

"Then here's what you are to do: Go to that place and take a piece of chalk along with you. Kneel down there, and with the chalk, draw a complete circle all around you. Then pray for God to send revival to everything inside that circle . . . and revival will begin with you."

What wise counsel. You see, we don't get revived by praying for everyone else's need for revival, though praying for others is both commended and commanded. True revival comes when we go to God in prayer and ask Him to remove, rekindle, restore, re-establish, and refurbish us. But I do warn you—revival may cost you *everything*.

Of the fifty-six men who signed the Declaration of Independence:

- Twelve had their homes ransacked and burned by the enemy.
- Nine fought and died from wounds or hardships.
- Two lost their sons in the war.
- One had two sons captured.
- Five were captured as traitors and tortured before they died.
- Numerous others lost all financial means, lived a life of hardship, and died in poverty.

What kind of men were they? Twenty-four were lawyers and jurists. Eleven were merchants. Nine were farmers and large plantation owners, men of means, well educated. Five were trained ministers. Four were physicians. One was a printer, another an iron worker, and one was a politician. But they signed the Declaration of Independence knowing full well that the penalty would be death if they were captured.

They signed and they pledged their lives, their fortunes, and their sacred honor. Can we, as soldiers and ambassadors of the cross, do any less?

Remember them, O my God, because they have defiled the priesthood and the covenant of the priesthood and the Levites. [31] *Remember me, O my God, for good.*

—Nehemiah 13:29, 31*b*

CHAPTER FIFTEEN

THE MAKING
OF A PEARL

Nehemiah 13

H ave you ever noticed how birthdays have a unique way of revealing our thoughts on aging? Do you realize that the only time in our lives when we liked growing older was when we were kids?

When you were less than 10 years old, you were so excited about aging that you used fractions. If someone asked you how old you were, you responded, "I'm five . . . and one-half!"

Then you hit double-digits and began dreaming of the next major milestone: 13. Oh, to be a teenager . . . *life will finally be all that I dreamed it would be.* Or so we thought.

When 13 finally got there, you immediately began skipping years. If someone asked how old you were, you said, "I'm almost 16." You might have two years to go, but that's completely ignored. You were *almost* 16.

Then 21 came and you'd really arrived—right? Even the words sounded like a ceremony: you became 21! But that didn't last very long. Soon you turned 30 and wondered where the time went. Next thing you know, you're pushing 40, and not long after, you reach 50.

Strange how we word this progression of time, isn't it? You *become* 21, *turn* 30, you're *pushing* 40, *reach* 50, and you *make it* to 60. By then you've built up so much momentum that you *hit* 70!

After that you're simply "in your 80s." But if you make it past that, you start going backward. You say, "I was just 92," or, "I was 95 last year."

Then a really strange phenomenon occurs: if you're one of the select few who make it to the century mark, you start thinking like a kid again. Someone asks how old you are and you say, "I'm one hundred and one-half . . . I'm *almost* 102!"

Yes, the aging process does give an interesting commentary on our view of life. We received a call from my wife's college roommate, and since Marsha wasn't home, her friend gave me the message that her son was engaged and going to be married.

I said, "How old is your son?"

She laughed and said, "He's twenty years old."

I said, "You're kidding; wait a second, we're too young to be *that* old."

She laughingly agreed.

How life changes. Sometimes the changes, pressures, and tribulations become so great that—whether thirty, forty, fifty, or sixty—you would like to once again be only five and one-half years old.

A letter sent to me reveals someone with just such a desire:

> I am hereby officially tendering my resignation as an adult. I have decided I would like to accept the responsibilities of a six-year-old again. I want to go to a McDonald's and think that it's a four-star restaurant. I want to see who can blow the biggest bubble. I want to think M&Ms are better than money because you can eat them. I want to drink Kool-Aid and eat Lemonheads with my friends. I don't want to change clothes because they get a little dirty, and I want to enjoy every day like it's summer vacation. I want to return to a time when life was simple. All you knew was to be happy because you were unaware of all the things that should make you worried or upset. I want to be excited about little things again, like my new Matchbox car or pogo stick. I want to live simply again. I don't want my day to consist of computer crashes, paperwork, cleaning, children, chores, depressing news, illness, and loss. I want to be in the roller derby and believe the Three Stooges are real. So, here's my checkbook and my car keys, my credit

cards and my 401(k) statements, my laptop, my iPad, my smartphone (okay, I'll keep that), my fax machine and, not least of all, my mortgage payment book. I am officially resigning from adulthood. And if you want to discuss this further, you'll have to catch me first because, "Tag, you're it, and you've got cooties." So, see you later, alligator!

Perhaps the words of this letter strike a similar chord in your own heart. Maybe you'd say, "I really *would* like to return to the simple life again—with no huge problems and no painful challenges. I want to live where the water is calm and the breeze is pleasant." However, as adults, we've learned by now that life is most often different from those simple desires. In fact, life is rarely simple. Even our Lord referred to each day being full of trouble *(Matthew 6:34)*.

Dr. Richard Seume, a man I had the privilege of worshipping under as he led the chapel services for Dallas Seminary, put an interesting perspective on the subject of not just growing older but on the ongoing troubles and pressures of life. Kent Hughes, in his commentary on James, quotes Dr. Seume's thoughts:

> Life on earth would not be worth much if every source of tribulation were removed. Yet most of us rebel against the things that irritate us, and count as heavy loss what ought to be rich gain. We are told that the oyster is wiser; when an irritating object like a bit of sand gets under the mantle of his shell, he begins covering it with the most precious part of his being—and he fashions a pearl. The irritation that it was causing is stopped by encrusting it with the pearly formation. Imagine that—a pearl is simply victory over tribulation.

Having contemplated aging and the troubles of life that never do seem to grow smaller or simpler, we come to the final chapter in the memoirs of Nehemiah . . . a time when the clock jumps forward more than a decade, and Nehemiah is now seventy years old. It is incredibly significant that God chose to close this dynamic book with Nehemiah, once again, handling pressure and tribulation. But this is reality and is a true picture of the Christian walk. It is not "happily ever after" on our pilgrimage through life—at least, not on earth, anyway.

Have you ever noticed that godly living is not simply gaining victory over a series of problems and then moving on to new ones. Sometimes it is battling the *same ones* over and over again. Nehemiah has only recently experienced great victory. He has cleaned up the city, rebuilt the walls, expelled the enemies, unified the nation, and brought the people through an extended period of revival. If there was ever a time when seventy-five-year-old Nehemiah should have resigned from the battles of life, it would be at this time of completion and victory. If there was ever a time when his aging body deserved a long rest in a cool place, it was *now*. Also, if there was ever a time when he might become disillusioned with the ongoing pressures and tribulations of life, it would be *now*. You would almost expect Nehemiah to say, "I'm going to resign from my well-worn post. I want life back like it was when I was a little kid. I'm tired of struggles. Give me that simple life again." But in the latter years of his life, just when you would expect him to walk away from trouble and sink into a rocking chair, he allows God to fashion yet another pearl. In his final journal entry, Nehemiah will reveal his greatest moments of faith and his most intimate moments with his divine Commander.

Before we begin one last look into this man's memoirs, let's consider two observations which come directly out of Nehemiah's own experience. These are realistic lessons about the Christian life:

1. **Your greatest test of faith is always the next one.**
2. **Your greatest display of character has yet to happen.**

So, don't rest on your laurels. Past victories do not guarantee future ones. Your greatest test, as a believer, is probably just around the corner. As we consider these last lessons from Nehemiah, the question is whether you will retreat from the hard work of the Christian life or whether you will fashion even more pearls for the glory of God.

PEARL MAKING 101

We are about to discover that the making of pearls is successful only if the intruding grains of sin are properly dealt with.

The Sin of Compromise

If you put the chronological pieces together, you discover that after Nehemiah had served as governor of Jerusalem for several years, he had then returned to serve King Artaxerxes in the palace. He was once again the king's cupbearer, just as he formerly had been. The only difference now is that Nehemiah is approximately seventy years old.

We are not sure how, but Nehemiah learns that his archenemy is gaining ground once again. Tobiah had been unsuccessful outside the city wall and was now at work *inside* the city wall. As hard as it was to imagine, verse five informs us that Nehemiah's old enemy has been given a suite of rooms *inside the temple itself.* An Ammonite was not allowed to enter the temple precinct—this was holy ground for priests only. Verse four reveals that the "deal" had been arranged by none other than Eliashib the high priest. How could this have happened? A key to this arrangement could be the simple fact that Eliashib was related to Sanballat. You may remember that Sanballat and Tobiah were friends and co-enemies of Nehemiah. Without a doubt, the high priest was consorting with the enemy—he had actually invited him into the temple to stay— and he was *compromising* the city.

One author said that inviting Tobiah to live in the Jewish temple was like inviting a fox to live in the chicken coop. Sometimes that is how the enemy of God's people works. Another author commented that even to this day, Satan does not always fight churches; sometimes he simply *joins* them.

Nehemiah's response to this arrangement reminds me of our Lord, who came into the temple precinct brandishing a whip. With it, He beat the Gentile merchants off the temple property, turning over their tables and chasing them out. Nehemiah was no less courageous:

> *It was very displeasing to me, so I threw all of Tobiah's household goods out of the room* [suite]. *Then I gave an order and they cleansed the rooms; and I returned there the utensils of the house of God with the grain offerings and the frankincense* (Nehemiah 13:8–9).

Can you envision this scene? As soon as Nehemiah uncovered the compromise, he threw out all of Tobiah's clothes, his furniture, his idols, his razor, and his toothbrush, too. He hauled it all out and then had the rooms ceremonially fumigated! One author suggested that it was as if Nehemiah didn't even want the *smell* of Tobiah lingering in the temple. Nehemiah handled this compromise in the same way he handled it in chapters four and six . . . *immediately!* There was no delay, no dialogue, and no devising a place for Tobiah to live. No, there was sin in the city and a sinner in the temple, and Nehemiah dealt with both in a decisive and swift manner.

May I remind you that today, in this dispensation of grace, *you are a temple of God* (1 Corinthians 3:16) and *your body is a temple of the Holy Spirit* (1 Corinthians 6:19). Has sin taken up residency in your temple? Have you set up a suite of rooms and invited sin to come live inside the holy temple of God? Have you secretly decorated some room in your heart and invited lust, pride, dishonesty, or some other sin to make itself at home?

Deal with any sin in the same way that Nehemiah dealt with compromise—*immediately* and *decisively*. Keep the temple of God clean!

The Sin of Selfishness

I also discovered that the portions of the Levites had not been given them, so that the Levites and the singers who performed the service had gone away, each to his own field (Nehemiah 13:10).

Stop for just a moment. Can you imagine how Nehemiah must have felt? I believe there is a volume of meaning behind the words **I also discovered**. Can you imagine how discouraging this must have been? In our study of **Nehemiah 10**, we watched as the Jewish nation signed a declaration specifically stating that they *would not withhold* their financial resources from the temple. And now, some years later, Nehemiah discovers they have not kept their word. Frankly, this hit him hard.

Nehemiah's feelings could be compared to:

- the teacher who uncovers the dishonesty of a favored student;
- the spouse who discovers the unfaithfulness of a mate;
- parents who find drugs stashed away in a drawer, while believing their son or daughter was "clean";
- the wife who stumbles on a bottle hidden in the closet after her husband promised he would never drink again.

Wham! These discoveries have a way of ripping into your heart. You want to run . . . you want to quit. Your soul hurts, and you don't know if you will ever again be able to breathe without that ache in your chest. You begin to pine for the days of a *simpler life*.

Nehemiah discovered the infidelity of God's people—their dishonesty and their selfishness. Instead of resigning, though, he buckles down for the long haul, and seventy years old or not, here he comes:

> *So I reprimanded the officials and said, "Why is the house of God forsaken?" Then I gathered them together and restored them to their posts. All Judah then brought the tithe of the grain, wine and oil into the storehouses* (Nehemiah 13:11–12).

In simple and direct words, he reprimands the leaders. They had allowed this to go on; they had turned a deaf ear and a blind eye to the unfaithfulness of the people. But he does not just *reprimand* the leaders, he *reinstructs* the people and then *restores* them to their original occupations of service. Then Nehemiah pleads with great fervor:

> *Remember me for this, O my God, and do not blot out my loyal deeds which I have performed for the house of my God and its services* (Nehemiah 13:14).

He seems to be saying, "O Lord, what am I going to do with these people? How agonizing, O God, to have to go back down this same path again. Lord, please don't forget what I'm trying to do here for Your sake and for the sake of Your glory." Unfortunately, that was not all Nehemiah discovered upon his return to Jerusalem.

The Sin of Materialism

While Nehemiah had been away, this sin had crept back inside the city gates:

> *In those days I saw in Judah some who were treading wine presses on the sabbath, and bringing in sacks of grain and loading them on donkeys, as well as wine, grapes, figs and all kinds of loads, and they brought them into Jerusalem on the sabbath day. So I admonished them on the day they*

> *sold food. Also men of Tyre were living there who imported*
> *fish and all kinds of merchandise, and sold them to the sons*
> *of Judah on the sabbath, even in Jerusalem. Then I repri-*
> *manded the nobles of Judah and said to them, "What is this*
> *evil thing you are doing, by profaning the sabbath day? Did*
> *not your fathers do the same, so that our God brought on us*
> *and on this city all this trouble? Yet you are adding to the*
> *wrath on Israel by profaning the sabbath." It came about*
> *that just as it grew dark at the gates of Jerusalem before*
> *the sabbath, I commanded that the doors should be shut*
> *and that they should not open them until after the sabbath.*
> *Then I stationed some of my servants at the gates so that no*
> *load would enter on the sabbath day* (Nehemiah 13:15–19).

You might notice further in verse 22 that Nehemiah prayed *after* he obeyed, not before. There are certain things you *do not need to pray about* before you do them. God has already spoken.

New Testament examples of this:

> *For this is the will of God . . . that you abstain from sexual immo-*
> *rality* (1 Thessalonians 4:3).

Immorality is the biblical word for any sexual relations outside of marriage. You do not need to pray about this. You do not need to ask God if there are any loopholes or extenuating circumstances, like "But we're engaged . . ." or "I love him" or "Everybody does it." God has already emphatically declared *His will* regarding this matter—now it is up to us to obey *His Word*.

> *Render to all what is due them: tax to whom tax is due . . .*
> (Romans 13:7).

Some of you may be thinking, "I'd prefer you keep talking about fornication; after all, I'm not guilty of that . . . let's skip past the *tax* issue." The truth remains—you don't have to get down on your knees sometime before taxes are due and pray, "Lord, is it Your will that I pay taxes?" He has already said that it is, and there are no loopholes around the will of God.

I love the way Nehemiah removes from the people of Jerusalem even the temptation to compromise with buying and selling on the Sabbath:

> *Once or twice the traders and merchants of every kind of merchandise spent the night outside Jerusalem. Then I warned them and said to them, "Why do you spend the night in front of the wall? If you do so again, I will use force against you." From that time on they did not come on the sabbath* (Nehemiah 13:20–21).

Even at his age, nobody wanted to tangle with Nehemiah.

> *And I commanded the Levites that they should purify themselves and come as gatekeepers to sanctify the sabbath day* (Nehemiah 13:22a).

What insight! Nehemiah dealt realistically with the problem. He told the Levites to continue doing their weekly assignments, but on the sabbaths, they were to perform a new assignment—keeping watch at the gates. His purpose for this new "job" was to protect the people by prohibiting the merchants from hanging around the city gates. Being a gatekeeper is the job description of every spiritual leader, including parents. This involves, as much as possible, even keeping *temptation* away from the family, the children, or the flock as best you can. *Gatekeepers must stay alert.*

We are confronted with at least *two thousand* commercials every day. Billboards, radio, television, magazines, newspapers, the internet—you name it. Your children alone are fighting their biggest battles as they learn what to listen to and what to ignore.

Years ago when our twin sons turned six years old, something interesting happened on their birthday. As usual, they received money from family and friends. They were sitting on the couch counting their loot when one of them announced, "I'm giving all my birthday money to church." We then glanced at our other son, awaiting the announcement of how he would spend his money. Without batting an eye, he said, "Not me, I'm spending all mine at the mall! I'm going to buy candy," he said. I remember looking back at my other son who was fidgeting around. You could almost see the battle going on inside him, and he finally admitted, "Well, I forgot all about that candy counter at the mall." What a great illustration for sixteen-year-olds, thirty-six-year-olds, and sixty-year-olds who want to make a spiritual commitment but then other voices are heard that make it tough to follow through.

What kind of gatekeeper are you in your own life? Gatekeeping is certainly a 24/7 job. Let one wrong thing in—even a little thing—and the city of your spirit is in danger of an enemy invasion.

The Sin of Disobedience

In those days I also saw that the Jews had married women from Ashdod, Ammon and Moab. As for their children, half spoke in the language of Ashdod, and none of them was able to speak the language of Judah, but the language of his own people (Nehemiah 13:23–24).

You may remember that as Ezra had stood and read the law *(chapter 8)*, most of the people could not understand Hebrew. For hours on end, Ezra and the priests explained the meanings of the words and, in essence, retaught the Hebrew language. Now, here in this chapter, the children are learning the language of their foreign Gentile mothers, and the Hebrew language is being ignored. The children were not being taught to read their national language. Nehemiah knew if they couldn't read Hebrew, they would not be able to read the *law of God*. Consequently, if they could not *read* the law, they would not be able to *obey* it. Not obeying God's law would lead them right back to where they were before rebuilding the walls—completely out of His will.

In a matter of only a few years, the people of God had moved from revival to rebellion. The astounding thing that we discover is *who* is in the middle of this turning away from God:

Even one of the sons of Joiada, the son of Eliashib the high priest, was a son-in-law of Sanballat the Horonite, so I drove him away from me (Nehemiah 13:28).

Did you recognize the names of Sanballat and Tobiah from previous chapters? Have you noticed how these names, like weeds in a garden, just keep cropping back up? It is not a coincidence. No, the enemy of our soul is relentless.

Josephus, the first-century Jewish historian, informs us that this grandson of Eliashib was named Manasseh. When Nehemiah kicked him out of Jerusalem, he immediately went to live with his father-in-law Sanballat in Samaria, and there established a false system of worship on Mount Gerezim.

This was the same false system for those people known as Samaritans. Therefore, the compromise that Nehemiah removed from Jerusalem eventually took root nearby. Nehemiah spotted the problem and the problem maker—and dealt severely with both. Donald Campbell, in his book *Nehemiah, Man in Charge*, writes:

> In these days when all areas of life are filled with confusion and are falling into disorder, we do well to subject our souls to the steadying, refreshing influence of a man like Nehemiah who was specific in his purposes toward God and who turned wishbones into backbones . . . we may believe that his influence ran down private channels in families and humble houses to the very time of the Messiah.

LESSONS FROM INTRUDING GRAINS OF SIN

God doesn't always provide final victory over some sins, but He does give *repeated* victory.

William Booth, the founder of the Salvation Army, was quoted by Warren Wiersbe in his book *Be Determined* as once saying to his staff: "I want you to always bear in mind that it is the nature of a fire to go out; you must keep it stirred and fed and the ashes continually removed for the fire to keep burning."

Temptation in the believer's life does not *diminish* with age, but rather, it grows more *deceptive* and *discreet*.

We must follow Nehemiah's example:

- Tackle compromise—*immediately*.
- Handle selfishness—*humbly*.
- Attack materialism—*realistically*.
- Deal with disobedience—*severely*.

During my weekly studies, I often enjoy reading and quoting from James Montgomery Boice. For many years, this man shepherded a church in downtown Philadelphia. His commentary on Nehemiah entitled *Nehemiah, Learning to Lead* has been a favorite of mine. He wrote in the final pages these words about the Christian life:

The Christian life is hard work. Even the Bible recognizes it as hard work by describing it as a battle (1 Timothy 6:12 – *Fight the good fight of faith . . .*); a race (2 Timothy 4:7 – *I have finished the* [race] *. . .*); a sacrifice (Romans 12:1 – *I urge you, brethren, by the mercies of God, to present your bodies a living and holy sacrifice, acceptable to God, which is your spiritual service of worship*).

Boice went on to conclude,

Bible study is hard. Prayer is hard. Witnessing is hard. Living a holy life in the midst of temptation is extremely difficult. Jesus Christ promised His followers not a comfortable life but a cross.

In other words, we cannot *resign* from trouble. We simply cannot go back to a simpler life. Instead, we must learn to tackle life as it happens, remove sin from our lives, and allow the Lord to make pearls of character from the many intrusions, troubles, and heartaches of this earthly pilgrimage.

Nehemiah comes to the close of his memoirs, and I find it interesting to read his final request of the Lord:

Remember me, O my God, for good (Nehemiah 13:31).

That is another way of saying, "Lord, I want to live life so that when You think of me, You will have good thoughts; when You observe my ways, my choices, and my lifestyle, You will be pleased with me." Ultimately, this was Nehemiah's greatest desire in life. That is the story of Nehemiah's heart, his faith, and his passion for God. But it has been more than just the story of a man's life. It has been the making of a beautiful pearl, and it's a demonstration of the only way to truly live.

What about *your* life? Are you allowing the Lord to make pearls or are you allowing the intruding grains of sin to have their destructive way within? Do you identify more with Nehemiah or with the people who had, once again, forgotten their commitments to the Lord? Who do you really *want* to be like? The same God who made a noble man of Nehemiah can make *you* a noble person, too. He has the remarkable pleasure of using *ordinary people* who are *wholly yielded to Him.*

Today, the world, the Church, and the family all need more ordinary people like Nehemiah—people who are willing to rebuild and restore their broken world.

People like you.

When you become just an *ordinary* person daily yielded to God, you begin to discover that He is making something *extraordinary* out of your life, as well.

Your memoirs will be worthy of writing . . . and reading.

SCRIPTURE INDEX